AYRTON
SENNA
A TRIBUTE

AYRTON
SENNA
A TRIBUTE
IVAN RENDALL

BCA

LONDON   NEW YORK   SYDNEY   TORONTO

This edition published 1994 by

BCA by arrangement with

PAVILION BOOKS LIMITED

CN 2894

Text © Ivan Rendall 1994

Designed by

The Bridgewater Book Company/Chris Dymond

Text research by Daniel Britten

Picture research by Julia Pashley

This book is typeset in Perpetua 11/14pt

Printed and bound by Butler and Tanner, Great Britain

CONTENTS

FOREWORD

I first met Ayrton Senna on a cold wet day at the Nurburgring in May, 1984. Mercedes had invited me to drive in a celebrity race which included nine world champions, past, present and future.

We drove matched Mercedes 190s. But out there in the cold rain, the youthful Ayrton ran away from us all and only Niki Lauda was able to mount any sort of a challenge.

That day I think we all realized we'd seen something rather special; and I certainly left Nurburg convinced that I'd seen a future world champion … and maybe a little more than that. History confirms that Ayrton Senna did indeed become a little more than that!

I wasn't close to Ayrton in the way that Gerhard Berger was close, but we were friends and I liked him.

We would exchange Christmas cards and our paths would cross; and when they did we'd talk the way friends do.

Visitors to my home often ask me just how highly I rated him. I show them my hallway. Along the wall hang two large signed pictures of racing drivers. One is Juan Manuel Fangio. The other is Ayrton. 'That's how high,' I say.

The word 'genius' is used rather carelessly these days; but a genius is undoubtably what he was. In the hands of a master such as Ayrton, the miraculous and the mundane can look deceptively similar. But I've seen him overtaking on the outside of a bend in heavy rain, and marvelled at a talent that was threatening to take car control across new horizons.

As a pure racing driver, he was virtually without flaw. A man who didn't have off days, who excelled on every type of circuit, in sunshine and in rain.

He had an all-consuming passion for motor racing, and for winning, that few men will ever know. It dominated his entire life and perhaps explains why the public were so slow to recognize his true worth both as a driver and a man.

Many accepted the image of a man constantly at war with his rivals; and preferred to choose more peaceful, more equable heroes.

And it was true. Ayrton could be difficult and he did occasionally do foolish things. But then men who care often do. However there were other qualities that few ever wrote about. He was totally loyal to his friends and to his family. He was honest to an unusual degree. And he could be touchingly kind, particularly to the younger drivers.

When Rubens Barrichello regained consciousness after his crash at Imola, he found Ayrton seated beside the bed. And recounts Rubens in some wonder, 'There were tears in his eyes.' Having known Ayrton, that doesn't surprise me at all.

To go ever faster, to constantly find new mountains to climb … this was an essential part of Ayrton's nature.

He knew he had been given a very special talent and he wanted the chance to display it to the world. He had always hoped that in the Williams he would be able to take the art of driving across new frontiers. It was then that fate dealt him the cruellest of hands.

Imola may have denied him his dream. But nothing can change what has gone before or wash away the memories. Ayrton can sleep in peace. He had already climbed the highest mountain.

Stirling Moss, July 1994

CHAPTER ONE

BLACK WEEKEND

The May Day holiday weekend of 1994 should have been a time of high hopes and expectations in motor racing. The arrival of the Formula One teams at Imola for the San Marino Grand Prix signalled the beginning of the European round of the World Championship, and the drivers, team bosses and fans would normally have been looking ahead to a summer of competition and spectacle. The sights and sounds were familiar – the sea of advertising, the shriek of engines – but the usually vibrant mood was missing. Nothing could lift the cloud which hung over Imola as the drivers prepared for the start, each dealing in his own way with the closeness of a rare visitor to modern racing – death.

Roland Ratzenberger, Formula One's newest recruit and driving in only his second race, had been killed in qualifying. His Simtek-Ford left the road at Villeneuve corner at around 190 mph, hitting a concrete wall nearly head on. Witnesses reported that part of the front wing had come off just before the crash, causing a sudden loss of downforce. Without this, the cornering speed was far too high, making the crash inevitable. Ratzenberger died from massive head injuries, the first death in Formula One for eight years, and the first on a race weekend for twelve years.

The normally tight safety regime at Grands Prix seemed suddenly rather ragged at the edges. Ratzenberger's death had followed a crash in the Friday practice session which left the Jordan-Hart driver, Rubens Barrichello, badly injured. As the weekend progressed there was increasing speculation that there was a problem caused by the new rules which governed the construction of the cars. The computers which controlled the active suspension and traction control systems had been banned, as had anti-lock

brakes. The changes had been introduced to put more emphasis on driver skill rather than technology, making racing more of a contest between men rather than cars. But the drivers had grown used to their computer aids, and doubts about the safety of the new cars were widespread.

Foremost among the doubters was Ayrton Senna. World Champion three times, in his eleventh season in Formula One, on pole position at Imola, he was acknowledged as the fastest, the most talented, and the most determined driver of the modern, high-tech age. With over a decade of Formula One racing behind him, he had the natural authority among the other drivers of being 'first among equals', and though he supported the idea of putting more emphasis on driver skills, he had made his views about the technical changes plain before the season started: 'It was a great error to remove the electronics… the cars are very fast and difficult to drive. Its going to be a season with lots of accidents and I'll risk saying we'll be lucky if something really serious doesn't happen.'

Senna visited the place where Ratzenberger had died. It was against the regulations, but he ignored them, he wanted to inspect the circumstances for himself and talk to the track marshals. Having done so, he decided not to take part in the final round of qualifying, and his team, Williams-Renault, with Benetton and Sauber-Mercedes, withdrew from the rest of the session as a mark of respect to Ratzenberger. Senna, and several other top drivers including his friend and former team mate, Gerhard Berger, now with Ferrari, and Michael Schumacher, of Benetton, discussed calling a drivers' safety meeting before the next Grand Prix at Monaco, to air their concerns.

Pacific Grand Prix, Aida, Japan, 17 April 1994: Ayrton Senna qualified for pole position in his second race in the Williams FW16, only to crash on Lap 1.

San Marino
Grand Prix,
Imola, 1 May
1994: Ayrton
Senna in
thoughtful mood
in the pits just
before the race.

If Senna was troubled for the state of the sport, he was also troubled in himself. Part of his aura was an extraordinary ability to isolate himself from any distractions in the build-up to a race, focusing his whole being on the single objective of winning. It made him self-absorbed, arrogant even, but through practice and qualifying, and at the start, he ruthlessly excluded any extraneous considerations, such as other people's feelings, as part of a very personal process of psychological preparation for winning. Yet behind the inscrutable mask he was human: the battered Rubens Barrichello was a fellow Brazilian and a close friend, and Roland Ratzenberger had been young and universally liked for his friendliness; when Senna heard of his death he cried. His powers of concentration were formidable, but completely excluding the events of the previous two days would have been impossible; psychologically, he was not as well prepared as he might have been.

He was also under other pressures. He had to prove to the world, and to himself, that he was still on top, and Imola was a crucial race in that process. He had failed to win a single point from the first two races of the season, having spun off both in his native Brazil and in Japan, and the team he had only just joined, Williams-Renault, was clearly not as dominant as they had been in 1993. On the grid next to Senna, 0.337 seconds slower in qualifying, was Michael Schumacher who had won both those races. He was leading the World Championship with maximum points and was widely tipped to take the 1994 title. His Ford-engined Benetton seemed to have the edge over Williams, and he was certainly Senna's nearest rival in skill.

The prospect of a close race between Senna and Schumacher, representing as they did, the old and the new, had been the subject of much pre-race speculation, and as Imola's starting lights turned to green, all eyes were on the two men. They lived up to expectations, charging away from the grid to get the best position at the first corner, when disaster struck the ill-starred race again. The Finnish driver, J J Lehto, stalled his Benetton on the line. He waved his hands frantically above his head to warn the other drivers, and most missed him, but Pedro Lamy was too late, and hit the Benetton hard in the rear, flinging debris into the grandstands. The mood turned to horror as nine spectators and a policeman were injured, fortunately none of them too seriously.

The chaos had hardly settled before Senna and Schumacher completed the first lap and came up to the start line at full speed. Surprisingly, the race had not been stopped. Instead, a safety car emerged from the pits, slowing the field right down, with the drivers holding their positions, until the track was cleared of debris. It took five laps, then the safety car left the track and the race was on again.

On Lap 6, going into Tamburello corner, Schumacher saw Senna's car step sideways slightly, moving off the racing line. Driving on instinct and with many years of experience, Senna corrected the 'nervousness' and came out of the corner on the line. Imola is a bumpy circuit, especially Tamburello, and Senna had spoken about the combination of the surface and its effect on his car in an interview with the German newspaper *Welt am Sonntag* before the race: 'It's one thing that's giving me a headache at the moment, because it exposes the weak points in my car which reacts nervously on this kind of race surface. This stems from the special aerodynamics and a difficulty in the suspension.'

On the next lap, Schumacher saw Senna's car step sideways again, and this time sparks flew as it 'bottomed out' at 192 mph. Any efforts Senna made to correct it were in vain. He braked, but the Williams went straight on, over a gravel trap, hitting the tyre stacks in front of a concrete wall at around 150 mph. Like Ratzenberger's crash, the impact was nearly head on, and Senna's car bounced off the wall and spun back on to the track.

The race was stopped. Fire crews and medical teams were on hand quickly to find that he had received massive head injuries, particularly to the forehead. A medical helicopter was brought in to airlift Senna to hospital in Bologna.

Even while he was in the air, news of the crash went round the world to millions of fans, but also to his family in Brazil and to his girlfriend, Adriane Galisteu, who was at Senna's home in Portugal. The news was confusing at first, for in the heat of the moment there had been misunderstandings. Bernard Ecclestone, Marketing Vice President of FIA, motor racing's governing body, and chairman of FOCA, the Constructors' Association, spoke to Leonardo Senna, Ayrton's brother, saying that he was dead. Then the information changed and Ecclestone reported to the family that Senna was alive but critically ill.

While doctors were trying to save Ayrton Senna's life, the race was restarted. In his commentary box, Alain Prost, a former team mate at McLaren and a bitter rival of his, cried while he described the scene for French viewers. Only hours earlier, in a rare moment of warmth after years of studied hostility, the two had shaken hands. To add further gloom to the day, a wheel came off Michele Alboreto's Minardi in the pit lane during the race, injuring four mechanics.

San Marino Grand Prix, Tamburello corner: Ayrton Senna's Williams just after impact with the wall; Ferrari's Gerhard Berger (right).

Michael Schumacher won the race, maintaining his perfect score in the World Championship, but there was to be no celebratory champagne on the rostrum, only a subdued and dignified reference to the hollowness of the victory.

At 6.40 pm, Ayrton Senna was pronounced dead. A shock wave hit the sport, a loss of confidence which rippled through the teams and the authorities. Tributes poured in from racing drivers round the world, both current and retired. The grief was genuine, but behind it controversy was soon bubbling as fundamental questions were asked: Were the cars safe enough? Was there something rotten at the heart of Formula One and the World Championship? If Ayrton Senna could die, then who was safe?

The debate was as old as motor racing itself, how to balance the needs of safety with the objective of winning. The computer aids which had been banned

The wrecked
Williams FW16:
Ayrton Senna
died from head
injuries caused by
suspension parts
attached to a
wheel which
came off on
impact.

were not there in the furtherance of safety, but in the interests of performance. Had Senna's car had all the aids, he would probably have been going faster. Against that, the argument was that there might have been a smaller possibility of it coming off the track, such are the fine tolerances constantly being adjusted from race to race. Imola is a very fast circuit, and to get the highest speed on the straights, downforce would have been set by all the teams as low as possible to maximize performance on the straights. But this is done at the expense of having it where it is needed, sticking the cars to the track on the corners. There is nothing new in this, it has been the case since the late 1960s when aerodynamics were introduced to produce a downforce, and in the final analysis, it is the driver, during practice and qualifying, who determines the balance between the two. It is the driver who opts for the fastest set-up who is going to win, and few drivers would opt for the less competitive, if safer, set-up.

Senna's car, like Ratzenberger's, was impounded by the Italian courts pending investigations. The circuit was closed to the public by a court order and notices were served on Imola's management that they were under investigation for culpable homicide.

As the teams packed up to go home, Damon Hill, Senna's team mate, said: 'It takes a weekend like this to scrape away that very thin veneer of apparent safety.'

Such had been the enormous strides in safety which had been made in motor racing in all formulas, that death, when it came, was a huge shock. It was the first death in Formula One since Elio de Angelis died testing for Brabham at the Paul Ricard circuit in France in 1986. Only two of the twenty-five drivers on the grid at Imola in 1994, Andrea de Cesaris and Michele Alboreto, had been racing the last time a driver had been killed in a race. That was in 1982 when RiccardoPaletti died in the Canadian Grand Prix. The last time the sport had lost one of its stars was in the Belgian Grand Prix earlier the same year when the Canadian driver, Gilles Villeneuve, crashed in practice.

Overcoming motor racing's greatest danger, the high-speed, high-impact crash, by making it survivable, had been one of the most significant developments of the 1980s. This was largely due to using technology borrowed from the aeronautical industry, in particular carbon fibre which was used to make the 'tubs', the slimline bodies which encased the drivers. There were also much larger gravel traps and run-off areas at most of the dangerous parts of the circuits, and modern Formula One had grown used to seeing drivers walk away from horrendous crashes.

Many of the drivers and spectators at Imola in 1994 would have remembered one of the most spectacular crashes at the very spot where Ayrton Senna had died. In 1989, Gerhard Berger's Ferrari went straight on, just like Senna's Williams, but it had hit the wall at a much shallower angle and tumbled along it, rather than bouncing back off it. Before it came to rest, it burst into flames, but fireproof overalls and swift action by the marshals had him out promptly with only burns to his hands. The following year at Monza, Derek Warwick crashed coming out of the famous Parabolica curve at Monza. His Lotus turned end-over-end, disintegrating as it did so, finishing upside down in the middle of the circuit. He climbed out and sprinted back to the pits to drive a spare car.

The crash which came closest to matching the shock of Senna's was Jim Clark's in 1968. Clark was acknowledged as the supreme driver of the period, but though his death in a Formula Two race at

Hockenheim was acknowledged as a tragedy for the sport, motor racing and death were closer partners in the 1960s and it was accepted as part of the drivers' risk. The nearest comparable accident in terms of its impact was thirty-nine years previously, in 1955, when a Mercedes driven by Pierre Levegh flew into the crowd during the 24-hour sports car race at Le Mans, and burst into flames, killing Levegh and eighty-one spectators. On that occasion, there were calls for motor racing to be banned, and it was in France for a time, while safety measures were improved.

By an almost sinister twist of fate, there were two other sporting deaths in Britain in the same week as the Imola tragedy – Bradley Stone, a young professional boxer, and Steve Wood, a jockey – and a debate started about the purposes of sport and the unacceptability of such danger. There were calls in the British press for motor racing to be made safer, if not banned. But others leapt to the defence of the sporting ideal, that these men chose to put themselves in danger, that they knew what they were doing and that without an element of danger, their sports would not have the huge followings they did have. Ayrton Senna was a hero to millions, but the price of that adulation was putting himself at risk. Perhaps one day motor sport will take place on computer terminals, but if that ever happens, it will have a different kind of hero.

It was not only the fact of the deaths of Senna and Ratzenberger which fuelled the debate, it was deeper than that. Did they die because of a rule change which had made the cars more dangerous in the interests of more exciting racing? Why was the race restarted? Was Senna dead before he went to the hospital, and did the authorities keep it secret so that the race would not have to be cancelled?

While doctors tried to save his life, Senna's colleagues continued to race, a move which was widely interpreted as callous, showing more concern for making money than for the dead. The editorials included one from the Vatican newspaper with the words: 'death itself was made into a brutal spectacle, the spark of the sponsors prevailed over death, silencing man'.

Motor racing had lost its king, but even before the funeral, the debate intensified, feeding on the atmosphere of controversy which is always bubbling in semi-secret just beneath the surface in the World Championship. The sport was suddenly washing its dirty linen in public: was the Formula One and World Championship establishment more concerned with making money than in the safety of the drivers?

With all the authority of four World Championships and the greatest number of Grand Prix wins in motor racing history, Alain Prost publicly criticized the rule changes, claiming that the stability of the cars had been sacrificed in the name of spectacle. Other theories about the cause of Ayrton Senna's death proliferated: Were cornering speeds too high? Should the computers have been banned? Did Senna's car pick up debris from the crash at the start?

The FIA instituted an enquiry, but no internal enquiries by the sport could be held while Senna's car, like Ratzenberger's, was impounded by the Italian authorities. The lack of any hard information fuelled further speculation. By the middle of the week, Patrick Head, Williams' technical director, was quoted in *Car Week* as saying that they thought Senna had 'lifted off a little' that caused a loss of downforce to the rear wing, which meant the car went straight on'. He later protested that his words had been taken out of context

and that Williams was 'still studying the data.'

Max Mosley, the President of FIA, the sport's governing body, criticized Prost for his statement about the rule changes, and rejected them, saying that there was no common factor in the five crashes at Imola. In defence of the decision to restart the race, Mosley used the same argument that had been used after the Le Mans crash in 1955: that it was dangerous to have hundreds of thousands of disappointed spectators leaving in a hurry at the same time. Cancelling the Imola race would have been unprecedented; when drivers have been killed in races, individual team managers have withdrawn as a mark of respect, but death has never caused the cancellation of a Grand Prix.

As the debate over decisions to continue the race taken on that fateful day at Imola and questions about the design of safety measures into circuits and the cars simmered on in Europe, so the luminaries of the motor racing world set out for Sao Paulo, for Ayrton Senna's funeral. If the shock wave caused by Senna's death had been severe in Europe, in Brazil it had hit the whole nation.

Ayrton Senna was a devout Christian. He died late on a Sunday in Europe, but before the end of the day, an open-air mass had been dedicated to him in his birthplace, Sao Paulo. President Itamar Franco caught the mood of the nation and quickly declared three days of national mourning, closing all state schools for the day of the funeral. Fighters of the Brazilian Air Force escorted the airliner carrying Senna's body home. A military honour guard placed his coffin on a fire engine for the journey to the Legislative Assembly where it would lie in state. Around a million people, most of them young, lined the expressway leading from the airport, as the cortege, escorted by a phalanx of police motor cycles, made its way through the outskirts of Sao Paulo. His fans followed the procession, their cars adorned with black flags and carrying photographs of their hero.

The outpouring of grief was spontaneous, real and nationwide. It was reflected on Brazilian television, in newspapers and magazines who responded to the nation's grief with special editions, tracing his career and listing his achievements, but also liberally spiced

with photographs of his many girlfriends. A hero had been killed and for many Brazilians, the thought that he had been to blame was unthinkable. That mood was reflected in the press, one magazine summing up in a single graphic what many felt was true: Senna in the position of the crucified Christ with a Formula One car as the cross. The implication was clear: somebody else was to blame for his death.

The loss was most deeply felt among young people. Brazil is a young, vibrant country, eager for a

Sao Paulo Legislative Assembly: the Lying in State of a patriot; Brazil's victory in the football World Cup three months later was dedicated to Ayrton Senna.

place in the world, but beset by economic problems. It has many problems and few heroes, but Brazil is a country which needs idols, be they politicians, Olympic medallists, soap opera stars or racing drivers. Ayrton Senna had all the ingredients of a Brazilian hero: he was young, handsome, at the peak of his powers, and he symbolized modernity. He had succeeded in the toughest of sports and he had made it on a world stage. Indeed, he was a global star with fan clubs across the world.

Senna was patriotic, an unofficial ambassador for Brazil. He wore the national colours on his racing helmet and they even adorned the wings of his model aircraft. Crucially, in a country where many of its most successful sportsmen chose to live abroad, whenever Senna was not racing, he returned to Brazil to recharge his batteries. In a country strongly divided by extremes of wealth and poverty, he was a truly national hero. He embodied a new spirit in Brazil, a bringing together of the elite, to which he had belonged all his life, with the masses who nevertheless adored him. During the emotionally charged period of mourning that followed Senna's death, there were several suicides: young people left notes saying that with Ayrton Senna gone life was no longer worth living.

Senna's body lay in state at the Sao Paulo Legislative Assembly, guarded round the clock by soldiers in ceremonial dress. On top of his flag-draped coffin rested his yellow and green helmet. A quarter of a million people filed past the coffin, ordinary people, state governors, old friends, children and members of Brazil's elite. Those who could not get in pressed up against the railings young girls with 'SENNA' written in felt pen on their foreheads and the national colours on their cheeks, edged with black.

Into this highly charged, very personal and thoroughly Brazilian expression of grief, came the great and the good of Formula One, some with bodyguards: Ron Dennis of McLaren, for whom Senna drove ninety-six Grands Prix and won three World Championships; Frank Williams in whose car he had died; Alain Prost, his greatest rival; his friend Gerhard Berger; Damon Hill, his team mate at Williams; and Rubens Barrichello, a fellow 'paulista' and a protégé of Senna's, who had recovered from his injuries. One of the last to arrive was Emerson Fittipaldi, another 'paulista' and, until the advent of Ayrton Senna, Brazil's greatest motor racing hero. Fittipaldi heard the news of Senna's death at a test session with his Marlboro-Penske Indycar team in the United States, and he admitted to being so shocked that he had to stop driving. He went home and cried for 24 hours. Of Senna, he said: 'Brazil has lost much more than the best driver in the world. We have lost a great man.'

The tributes from drivers round the world continued. Stirling Moss called him 'the greatest driver of our time' and Niki Lauda agreed, adding 'when someone like him is killed you have to ask what is the point of it all'.

Alain Prost, a great rival, vowed at the funeral that he would not sit in a Formula One car again. 'He was a master of his craft. I was proud to race against him.'

They were prominently quoted in Brazilian newspapers, leaving no doubt among his countrymen, that among his peers in motor racing, he was regarded not only as the best racing driver of the age, but possibly of all time.

A notable absentee was Nelson Piquet, also a Brazilian, and also a three-times World Champion. Piquet and Senna were not only rivals, they had traded

insults down the years. Piquet had once described Senna as 'the Sao Paulo taxi driver'. There was a personality clash between them, an antipathy, going back at least a decade, rooted in the politics of Formula One and in rivalry for sponsorship in the top Formula One teams. The day after Senna died, Piquet wrote a warm tribute to Senna in the *Jornal da Tarde*, highlighting their brotherhood as Brazilians, while acknowledging their differences.

Another absentee was Bernard Ecclestone, President of FOCA, the teams' own body, and a vice-president of FIA. He went to Brazil, but the Senna da Silva family let it be known that he would not be welcome at the funeral. Ecclestone had been in charge at Imola and there was still real resentment at the way the crash, Senna's death, and the restart of the race had been handled.

The funeral procession brought Sao Paulo to a standstill. The Senna da Silva family led the way, his mother Neide with whom he had been exceptionally close, his father Milton, his elder sister Viviane who was also very close and his younger brother Leonardo, who was one of his business managers. Next to Viviane, holding hands, was Xuxa Menguel, the beautiful Brazilian television presenter who had been Senna's girlfriend in 1990. There had been talk of marriage; a union which would have had not only the family's blessing, but that of most of Brazil, the coming together of a national hero and heroine. They parted, but Xuxa was still a close friend of the family, closer in fact than Adriane Galisteu, the model with whom Senna was sharing his life when he died: she was not part of the family party.

The pallbearers were drawn from the top echelons of Formula One, highly recognizable, but curiously

Sao Paulo, Brazil, 5 May 1994: the city came to a halt as army cadets carried Ayrton Senna's coffin to its final resting place.

21

A mother's grief:
Neide Senna da
Silva, leading
her family's
mourning at her
son's funeral.

unfamiliar in their sombre suits and sad faces. Rarely can his colleagues have been as close to him in life as they were in death; most had memories of incidents with Senna, both off and on the track, some of latter which put their lives in danger. Despite the rivalry and the politics, among drivers in Formula One there is a close fraternity, an exclusive club of men who are drawn together by the shared experience of danger, of driving at and beyond the limit, of having been at the edge in motor racing and survived.

At the graveside, Brazilian soldiers fired three volleys of blanks while above, the Brazilian Air Force put on a display of smoke trails, painting a giant S in the sky surrounded by a huge heart.

The funeral over, the debate over safety resumed. In Britain it reached the correspondence columns of *The Times* where a reader criticized safety in Formula One. This prompted Max Mosley to reply, pointing out that concrete walls were permitted where the likelihood was that in an accident the angle would be shallow, and the deceleration slower, than when the impact was head on. Senna, he continued, had most likely been killed by a blow to the head from one of the front wheels which had come off the car on impact with the wall.

Behind the debate was the knowledge that the next Grand Prix was at Monaco. Monaco is the social heart of the World Championship, it is the premier race, its parties the best, and the patronage of Prince Rainier gives it both an added tone and a link with the past of motor racing. The first Monaco Grand Prix was in 1929, and in the 1990s, it is an anachronism. There are no sand traps on the winding street circuit, drivers are hemmed in by solid walls and Armco barriers. They are rarely able to use full power for high speed,

but it remains in the World Championship calendar, and few in the sport would have it any other way.

Ayrton Senna had won at Monaco six times, a record, and his loss was keenly felt. The Formula One family was still in mourning and it was examining itself to the extent that at one meeting, the FIA had considered cancelling the race, and the rest of the season. The proposal had been quickly rejected and Ayrton Senna's and Roland Ratzenberger's names were invoked in support of the view that racing must go on. It was the only way that confidence could be fully restored.

In a hundred years of motor racing, there have been many serious crashes and when they happen, especially when they are fatal, the authorities of the day have tried to reduce speed and power. But the response from the designers, engineers and drivers is equally predictable, they want to win and they have always found ways of bringing speeds back up again. Treating motor racing as a laboratory for the motor car industry by improving engineering standards has been the central rationale behind the sport for a century, and while it sometimes seems remote from the idea of a family car, the links are still there in such areas as tyre and brake technology.

The FIA had to introduce change without emasculating the sport. The first new rules announced were in the pit lane where a speed limit of 50 mph was introduced and the number of mechanics limited, banning them unless they were working on a car. Design changes to the cars which were in the pipeline for 1995 – aimed to reduce downforce, power and speed, and to reduce cornering speeds by up to a third by stepping the underside of the car – would be brought forward and measures such as airboxes which

In life, Ayrton
Senna and his
elder sister,
Vivianne, were
very close; they
shared a great
sense of family
and a strong
Christian faith.

funnel air into the carburettor would be banned. The special fuels which the teams used were also banned; they had to use regular pump fuel.

The days leading up to Monaco were tense. Gerhard Berger was visibly shaken by the events at Imola and there was speculation that he would give up racing, but he overcame the psychological barrier and took part. Williams decided to field only one driver, Damon Hill, in the race as a mark of respect. Ratzenberger's team, Simtek, did the same. In an ironic twist of fate, Damon Hill would have to carry the burden of re-establishing the morale of his team as his father had done at Lotus when Jim Clark died at the wheel in 1968. Instead of filling the two spaces from the other teams, it was decided that the two spaces on the front of the grid would be left vacant as a mark of respect to Senna and Ratzenberger.

The brittle nerves of the race organizers and the drivers were made more fragile when the Sauber-Mercedes driver, Karl Wendlinger, crashed badly in practice and was rushed to hospital where he lapsed into a coma. Sauber-Mercedes pulled out of the race as the doubts and the questioning headlines returned. But despite much hand-wringing in the press, there was never any real doubt that the race would happen. The people in Formula One are tough. To get to the top takes a hard and ruthless streak, and the collective resolve and nerve of the drivers, though it may have wobbled slightly, held firm.

The mood on race day was sombre, but purposeful. The usual round of parties had been very subdued, and as a reminder of what had happened only two weeks previously, all along the route there were improvised banners with Ayrton Senna's name hanging from windows and among the crowds lining the circuit.

But even the spectators were subdued, adding to the general mood of uncertainty; it was almost as if Senna was somehow still there, or would soon arrive. The feeling of personal loss went far beyond those who were racing; when the BBC television commentator, Murray Walker, read a statement from the Senna da Silva family, his voice broke with emotion.

The drivers' own tribute came just before the start when they assembled for a minute's silence, holding a Brazilian flag for the photographers and television cameras with the words 'Adeus Ayrton' across it. It was a genuine mark of sorrow and respect, but it was also an awkward moment, many of the drivers looked uncomfortable participating in such a public display of emotion just before a race, and the silence was broken by engines being warmed up in the background.

Behind the public sombreness and the rituals of respect for the dead, motor racing was getting back to its roots in competitiveness. Michael Schumacher took pole position for the first time in his career with a stunning 1 minute 18.5 seconds, breaking Senna's lap record for the circuit and there was an unmistakable sense that the baton of greatness, of being 'the man to beat' was passing to the 25-year-old German driver. He was undoubtedly the prince, if not yet the king.

The downbeat mood was broken by the start. Engines roared confidently and commentators built up swiftly to their usual pitch of excitement, conveying a feeling of a return to business as usual. They held their breath for a second as Damon Hill and Mika Hakkinen collided on the first corner, putting both of them out of the race, but resumed with vigour when it was plain they were safe. The result was a coronation for Schumacher who won again, giving him a perfect 40 points in the World Championship from four races.

Monaco, 15 May
1994, the first
Grand Prix
without Ayrton
Senna for a
decade: Formula
One drivers pay
silent tribute
before the race.

Even with Karl Wendlinger still in a coma, Formula One seemed to be regaining its confidence.

As the teams prepared for the next Grand Prix two weeks later in Spain, the team bosses locked horns with the governing body over the new rules. They protested that they could not introduce the changes to their cars in time, and exerted pressure to delay them; a compromise was worked out.

Williams replaced Ayrton Senna with their test driver, David Coulthard, who would be driving in his first Grand Prix. Schumacher looked like winning another easy race until he lost everything except fifth gear and Damon Hill passed him to win, boosting morale at Williams. But with Schumacher just 7 seconds behind, even his second place showed he had the mark of a great driver in the making.

A week after the Spanish Grand Prix, Karl Wendlinger came out of his coma and began speaking with relatives. With Michael Schumacher filling the void at the top of the sport, the wound in the body politic of Formula One was healing well, but without Senna, there was something missing on the circuit – the fierce, unbridled, close competition between drivers – the lifeblood of motor racing. Schumacher and Benetton looked unbeatable, and the motor racing press was soon speculating on the return of Nigel Mansell to Formula One to inject some much needed spectacle into the racing. Mansell had switched to Indycar racing after winning the 1992 World Championship for Williams. In 1993, he won the Indycar title, the first driver ever to win both championships back-to-back, and he was fully committed to defending his title with the Newman-Haas team. The language of such deals is money.

Mansell would not be able to race in all the Grands Prix because of his commitments to Indycar, but negotiations between Mansell and Williams reached serious levels and although the amounts were never disclosed they were obviously formidable. It was some measure of the importance of Senna in making Formula One the spectacle it was.

Mansell did return with Williams – for the French Grand Prix, causing a stir of publicity – a measure of the extent to which racing drivers had become global stars. Refreshingly, however, his return was seen to be against the grain of motor-racing history; Mansell is a part of the past in Formula One. The void which Ayrton Senna left will be filled, not by stars making 'guest appearances' but by new driving talent coming up, with the hungry, thirsty and blood-red will to win, which was Senna's hallmark.

What will never be replaced was Ayrton Senna's enigmatic character which drew as much attention, often more, than his driving skill. He was an unusual man by any standards, a twentieth-century hero who obviously drove for the sheer excitement and love of it, but who used it ruthlessly to make money; he died leaving an estate of around $180 million built on his name and his extraordinary popularity. Senna was a mass of contradictions. In racing, he was ruthless, but he was also a devout Christian. He was deeply private, yet he used his image to launch all manner of businesses, from a comic strip character based on himself called 'Senninha', to mountain bikes and an Audi distribution network. He made donations to charity, but on the understanding that they were never publicized. The key to the duality of his personality, to the hard man and the soft man, is in Ayrton Senna's homeland, in Sao Paulo, Brazil.

Thousands of 'paulistas' were unable to get into the Legislative Assembly to pay their last respects to the local hero, so they grieved outside instead.

CHAPTER TWO

THE BOY FROM BRAZIL

Brazil is the fifth largest country in the world. In European terms, if one end of it was in London, the other would be in Tehran. It is a country full of promise, but with problems to match: 5% of the population owns 80% of the land and 10% of the population earns 50% of the income. For years, it has been trying to sustain an almost feudal social

system in the countryside, while moving from the third to the first world by industrializing and embracing new technologies.

The engine of that economic change is Sao Paulo, today the most populous city in the world, with over 15 million people. It is a place that has grown huge from migration from the vast countryside of Brazil, as people search for work and a better life in an industrial town. Consequently it is a vibrant place and a place of extremes of wealth and poverty, a flashy example of Brazilian culture: brash, dynamic, with a high value on machismo.

Sport has a central place in Brazil's popular culture, particularly football, but a close second is motor-racing with its high-tech overtones and symbols of modernity. The highly developed amateur karting and saloon car-based motor racing championships in Brazil have produced a disproportionate number of racing drivers, many of whom have made the pilgrimage to Europe in order to move into Formula One and international competition. Brazil has also produced more than its share of multiple Formula One World Champions: Emerson Fittipaldi, Nelson Piquet and Ayrton Senna.

Ayrton Senna was born on 21 March 1960, the second child of Milton Guirado Theodoro da Silva and his wife Neide. His mother's maiden name was Senna, and the full family name was Senna da Silva. It was a wealthy family, with a lovely family home in the northern Sao Paulo suburb of Santana, well away from the teeming 'favelas', the shanty towns. The family wealth was based on a car components business which employed 750 people, on a drinks distribution business, and on land in the gorgeous hinterland of Sao Paulo State, where ten cattle farms covered 400,000

Ayrton Senna da Silva, aged 4, with his first car; he grew up fascinated by the range of family cars and farm vehicles connected with the family businesses.

hectares on which Milton da Silva, Senna's father, raised some 10,000 head of cattle.

By any standards, it was an idyllic existence for a child, an Ivy League family, where security, private education, servants, health, and cars to explore the wide open spaces and the family farms were all taken for granted. The Senna da Silva family was close, loving and devout, and the young Ayrton, with an elder sister Viviane and a younger brother, Leonardo, wanted for little. Ayrton Senna da Silva grew up expecting a lot from life, in a country with a lot to offer, and the seeds of a pampered, even spoilt, childhood were there in abundance.

He was a good-looking child in a country where looks count for a lot, but he was physically uncoordinated and awkward in his early years. A neurologist diagnosed a motor coordination problem: his mother often had to buy him two ice creams at once since he invariably dropped the first on the ground; and walking up three steps at a time was a task he had to concentrate hard to achieve.

Neither was he a particularly good student. In his early school days he was hyperactive and known as 'the rocket' for his behaviour outside classes, at playtime. He was also introverted, quite content with his own company, making few friends. He lived through cars, they had been his passion from a very young age and here again his family rather than his school provided what he wanted. As the owner of a car components business, his father had the means to build him a customized 1 hp kart and, at four, he was given the dream toy. Behind a steering wheel he was a different boy: focused, alert, attentive and coordinated, he would spend every weekend driving his kart at home and in the local parks. Driving was an outlet for his

energy and he showed an extraordinary level of application at something he wanted to do and at which he was good. His school work inevitably suffered.

His father used the conventional tool of denying him his beloved toy if his school reports were not good enough. Senna was intelligent and did just enough to keep going, judging his father's requirements just right in order to get what he wanted. At the age of seven, Milton found him driving the farm jeep unaided. He was too small to operate the clutch so he changed gear simply by listening to the engine noise, changing up or down when the revs sounded right.

His knack of getting what he wanted was used on his mother too. Neide Senna da Silva more than once turned a blind eye when he took the family car out on the road at the age of eight, even once when he was caught by the police.

Milton da Silva was a motor racing enthusiast and he followed the fortunes of the sport as it went through great changes in the 1960s, just at the time when young Ayrton was indulging his obsession with cars. Britain was taking the lead in motor racing, challenging the old firms of Ferrari and Maserati, and two names stood out from all the rest: Jim Clark and Lotus. Senna's first impressions of motor racing came through following the fortunes of a highly gifted driver in a glamorous world many miles away. Senna wanted to be like Jim Clark, the hero of Formula One, and when in the 1960s Milton promised young Ayrton a full-sized kart when he was ten, he added the encouraging thought that he might indeed be a champion like Clark one day.

With the advent of sponsorship, advertising and televised motor racing, the sport became a part of the wider, popular, international culture, making it very attractive and quickly absorbed in a society such as Brazil, where male machismo, good looks and sporting achievement are highly prized.

Motor racing quickly became a passion for Senna, but in Brazil it was still a dreamworld based in way-off Europe – a distant business with strange names like Lotus, Brabham, Tyrell, McLaren and March. When Jim Clark was killed in 1968, Jackie Stewart took over his position as the international idol, becoming World Champion in 1969.

In 1970, not only motor racing but success on a world stage was suddenly brought to Senna's doorstep. Emerson Fittipaldi, the son of a Sao Paulo sports journalist, who had started his career in karts on the same tracks as Ayrton, had gone to Europe and taken on the Europeans at their own game. He had joined Colin Chapman's Lotus as second driver to Jochen Rindt who had replaced Jim Clark. But Rindt was killed at the 1970 Italian Grand Prix at Monza and Fittipaldi was suddenly moved into the top slot at Lotus having driven in only three Grands Prix. He more than rose to the occasion, and quickly confirmed his position at Lotus, restoring morale with a superb victory at the next race, the United States Grand Prix at Watkins Glen. Fittipaldi was an instant hero in Brazil, particularly in Ayrton Senna's bedroom where a poster joined Stewart's on the bedroom wall.

With his head full of dreams of becoming a second Fittipaldi, Ayrton celebrated his tenth birthday and his father presented him with a full-sized kart with a 100 cc Parilla engine. Ayrton was not old enough to race it, the legal limit being thirteen, but he went on practising, perfecting a natural ability at home and on a kart circuit at the Parque Anhembi where other rich young 'paulistas' raced.

Ayrton Senna da Silva went to the Rio Bronco secondary school, and year by year, did just enough to scrape through his exams. His physics teacher remembers him sitting at the back of the class, drawing racing cars and looking at photographs of races. He was a serious boy, a seriousness which suggested a maturity beyond his years, and he had few friends, either at school or among those he met through karting. His mind was on the international motor racing circuit with Fittipaldi and Stewart.

In 1971, Jackie Stewart won the World Championship. Then in 1972, Brazil held its breath as the quiet, thoughtful Emerson Fittipaldi, driving Colin Chapman's classic Lotus 72D, challenged Stewart for the World Championship. Fittipaldi won five Grands Prix to Stewart's four to become the youngest ever World Champion at the age of twenty-five. Motor racing fever swept Brazil and, in 1973, there was even more reason to celebrate when the Formula One circus came to Brazil for the first ever Brazilian Grand Prix. Young Ayrton Senna could barely believe his luck when it was announced that the race would be run at Interlagos, just outside Sao Paulo.

Emerson Fittipaldi and his elder brother Wilson both took part and Emerson won. With Brazil's own hero winning in his home town the country went wild with enthusiasm; here was something which Brazil could be proud of, and boys all over the country aspired to be like Emerson Fittipaldi.

Fittipaldi did not win the world title again that year, but he did in 1974, this time for McLaren. With two victories South America had a motor racing hero in the making who could be put alongside the great Argentinian, Juan Manuel Fangio, who had won five World Championships in the 1950s.

Just weeks after the heady experience of the Interlagos Grand Prix, Ayrton Senna da Silva had his thirteenth birthday; he could race karts legally. He approached Elcio de Sao Thiago who ran a kart racing club in Lapa. In preparing for his first race, Thiago saw a nervous boy, always looking over his shoulder for the competition, but his first full race at the hallowed Interlagos kart track, near the Grand Prix circuit, on 1 July was a triumph.

Karting had a substantial following among the young boys who could afford it, and one of the fastest among the Sao Paulo karters was Maurizio Sala. He was 'the boy to beat', the habitual winner, and had won the races leading up to Interlagos. The race was a battle between Sala's experience and all the pent up competitiveness in Ayrton Senna da Silva which had been waiting for just that moment. Senna won, demonstrating a will and a determination to win, matched by the natural ability and aggressiveness to do so. Sala and the other kart drivers freely recognized from that race on that Senna was exceptional.

Sala and Senna crashed together frequently and the karting fraternity quickly found out that even at thirteen he was completely fearless on the circuit. He would not give way to anybody, yet he expected others to give way to him. Nothing intimidated him; once he was out in front, getting past was difficult. In the rain, he was even more formidable, his touch was so sure; the wet seemed to have no effect on his driving.

Kart racing is an ideal training ground for racing drivers. Karts are small and very positive, almost strapped to the driver's back, and it is close racing, very competitive. It is much slower than car racing, but it is dangerous; in the 1970s, one or two drivers would be killed each year. In later years Senna

described it as more competitive than any other form of racing, and he acknowledged that he learned the basic skills and instincts of a racing driver on karts.

For all the material and psychological support of his family and its wealth, he had a precocious and prodigious talent. The uncoordinated young boy had turned into a highly focused and very able driver. He knew about one thing: winning, and all his faculties

Loving father: Milton da Silva with Ayrton in 1973. The affection of his family gave him a lifelong confidence.

were aimed at that. From an early stage, he sublimated his school work and his social life to that end. Where Maurizio Sala was gregarious, Senna was introverted and shy. Sometimes Senna would visit the Sala home with other young people, and he even went out with Sala's sister, Carolina, for a time. But he was awkward with people, and very serious; any relationship had to come second to his kart racing, and the relationships did not last. He was uncomfortable in crowds and did not join in group activities, but this standoffishness, though it made him few friends, earned him the respect of those against whom he raced. It set him apart, made him somewhat mysterious; other drivers wondered about him and that uncertainty gave him a certain psychological edge. When Maurizio Sala described him as 'sensational, half wild', it says more about Sala's position in their relationship than it does about Senna.

Focus of attention: from his earliest experiences in racing, Ayrton Senna developed a way of securing the support of anybody around him who could help him win.

Senna's ability to impose his quiet authority on a situation, and get his own way, was a crucial ingredient in his success on the track. It showed in the way he prepared for a race, which was meticulous, perfectionist and selfish. Most of the Sao Paulo karting fraternity used the workshops of a Spanish engineer, known as Tche. Most made and tuned their own engines under his guidance, but Tche made Ayrton Senna's engines personally, and when he arrived at the track in a chauffeur-driven van for which his father picked up the bill, the psychological advantage grew. He looked unbeatable, and he learned from an early age the psychological advantage that gave him.

In 1977 he moved up to international kart racing which took him all over South America, and in Uruguay that year he won the South American Kart Championship. On the international circuit he met Mauricio Gugelmin, a fellow Brazilian, who became one of Senna's small circle of close friends.

The following year, he won the South American title again, and this time he took the Brazilian Championship as well, but his eyes were really set on 1978 World Kart Championship which was being held at Le Mans in France in September. He contacted the top Italian kart builders DAP, in Milan. The company had its own team of professionals, but it also took on amateurs who could pay. A price was agreed; Milton paid up and Ayrton set off for Italy alone with only a smattering of Italian and English, the international language of motor racing.

It was a cruel baptism into the nomadic world of international motor racing for an eighteen-year-old. He was used to being on the move, and away from the embrace of his family, but in South America he was never far from home and those around him spoke the

World Kart Championships, Le Mans, 1978: Ayrton Senna's first taste of international racing.

Ayrton Senna da Silva, aged 18: widely acknowledged as a highly gifted kart driver, he was also impatient, sometimes so eager to win that he crashed.

same language. But he knew what he wanted and he was prepared to go through with it to win, and he became hardened to the rigours.

He went to Parma for three weeks test driving before the championship, and to meet the stars of the DAP team, an Englishman, Terry Fullerton, and the Dutchman, Peter Koene. Both men were used to rich young South Americans who could pay their way, but they rarely expected much of them. They recognized him as quick, and he had obvious ability, but they also saw that he was very immature, too eager to be fast. Using schoolboy English, he sought their advice and they told him he was trying too hard, throwing the kart about too much, sliding into the corners, effectively killing off his speed.

In the early races of the World Championships at Le Mans he showed that he was no mere rich young South American by winning two of the early heats; he then retired from the third with a seized engine. The competition was a good deal fiercer than in Brazil and in the three races which constituted the final, he came seventh in the first, collided with Mickey Allen, an Englishman, in the second, then came

sixth in the third, finishing sixth overall in the Championship. For a new face it made the other drivers and the press take notice. *Karting* magazine described his performance as 'sensational'.

Senna would not have agreed; he was not racing to take part, he was racing to win, and he was not used to being beaten. Far from putting him off, coming sixth only prompted him to want to win in Europe all the more. In 1979, he won the Brazilian Championship again, then he went back to Europe for a longer season starting at Jesolo, near Venice. Next to the World Championships which that year were being held at Estoril in Portugal, the Jesolo meeting was the most competitive, and a good preparation. He had not changed very much from the previous year, he still had an abundance of ability and courage, hampered by a lack of polish and experience. The hallmark of his technique was to go out every time to win, never mind if it was practice, testing or qualifying. He had to be in front, and set the fastest time, even when it was not important tactically. Out on the track he would rarely sacrifice speed for holding off and gaining a greater understanding of just how to set up the kart and just how to tackle each corner. He tried too hard, he was too eager, and sometimes the sheer will to win prevailed over a fuller appreciation of how best to go about it, especially against drivers with huge experience of racing on their own home ground.

His approach nearly caused disaster in the last test session at Jesolo. The track was getting steadily stickier as the karts deposited rubber on the surface, and he failed to appreciate that he would have to set the kart up differently. Going into a fast corner, the two inside wheels lifted off and he was thrown out of the kart at around 50 mph into an iron fence, the kart then hitting him from behind.

He was badly shaken but not seriously injured and took part in the championship. But he was not on his usual form, the experience had affected him. In the final he tried very hard; too hard again as it turned out. Attempting to overtake on the inside, he crashed, though he still managed to come sixth overall.

At Estoril for the World Kart Championships, at least he was at home among Portuguese speakers, and he had the crowd behind him. In the third semi-final, he was lying in second place, racing wheel to wheel with Terry Fullerton who was widely regarded as the best kart driver of the day. Senna only needed to come second to take pole position in the first final, but that iron determination to win rather than play safe and back off, gripped him, and he gave Fullerton a race. At a crucial moment, Fullerton's engine seized, and they came together and crashed. Senna's kart turned over, but undaunted, he righted it and raced on, coming eleventh.

There were three finals: Senna led in the first, to the enormous joy of the crowd, but steadily the more experienced drivers overhauled him and he finished

fifth. In the second, he worked his way through the field to lie second, behind the Dutchman Peter de Bruyn driving a Hutless-Parilla. Then de Bruyn's chain broke, leaving Senna in the lead until his DAP team mate, Peter Koene passed him to win. Senna won the third race to a rapturous reception, putting him on the same points as Koene over the three races. To break the tie, the winner was decided on their placings in the semi-finals and now Senna's eleventh place following his crash with Fullerton counted against him and the title went to Koene. Senna was upset. He had been beaten by a hair's breadth, and he did not like it.

In 1980 he won his third Brazilian Championship, then moved on for a third attempt at the world title at Nivelles in Belgium, but he could not improve on the previous year, coming second again.

He was nineteen years old and his life was at a watershed. He wanted to be a racing driver, and he was tantalizingly close, but the next stage would be very expensive and his father was not overwhelmed by the plan. He wanted his son to become part of the family business, and when he returned to Brazil, Ayrton went to business school in Sao Paulo. His attendance lasted three months. He dropped out, having persuaded his father to back him financially for a full year in Formula Ford in Britain.

The decision to go on racing was complicated by having a wife. The shy boy had married a beautiful girl from a prominent Brazilian family, Lilian Vasconcelos de Souza, and the newly-married couple left sunny Sao Paulo for cold and windy Norfolk in the middle of an English winter. They rented a bungalow near Snetterton, home of the Van Diemen Formula Ford 1600 racing team run by Ralph Firmin. In joining Van Diemen, he was following in the footsteps of fellow

Townsend Thorensen Formula Ford 1600 Championship, Donington, 15 August 1981: Ayrton Senna at the start in the Van Diemen RF81-Ford; he won.

'paulista', Carlos Pace, one of the first to follow Fittipaldi to Britain to get into the big time. More recently, two other Brazilians, Roberto Moreno and Raul Boesel, had passed through Van Diemen, and both were having considerable success driving in Formula Three in 1981.

The 1.6 litre Formula Ford cars represented the first rung on a ladder which led via their two- and three-litre equivalents to Formula One. They were real racing cars capable of around 125 mph and were tricky to handle, but Senna took to them quickly, analysing each corner and discussing it later. He was analytical, but he was as impetuous as ever too, and brought with him all the aggressiveness and the need to be in front at all times which had been the hallmark of his karting career. The Formula Ford cars were much faster than karts, but within a few laps, he was handling them calmly and with self-assurance. To be able to talk to the mechanics after the race, he developed a way of thinking in English when he had to discuss it later, while still thinking in Portuguese when it was purely for himself.

There were three championships run for Formula Ford 1600 in Britain, two sponsored by the ferry companies P & O and Townsend Thorensen, and one by the RAC. Senna's first race was at Brands Hatch on 1 March in the P & O Championship. He qualified half way down the grid which was good for a newcomer who had not raced at Brands Hatch before, and made a good start. In the race he came in for some criticism for being too wild, but he pushed hard for all twelve laps, finishing fifth, 8 seconds behind the winner, Enrique Mansilla. *Autosport* magazine noted his impressive debut with the prophetic line: 'undoubtedly we shall hear more of this young man.'

He decided to concentrate on just two championships, the Townsend Thorensen and the RAC, and at Thruxton a week later he was third, taking his first points in the Townsend Thorensen Championship. A week after that, still two weeks short of his twenty-first birthday, he was back at Brands Hatch for another in the series. For his second drive at Brands, Van Diemen gave him their new car and, though he had only raced there once before, he knew the circuit much better now and surprised a few people by taking pole position. It was a wet day, and those who had been surprised were soon astonished, for in the wet he was even more impressive. He had such sensitivity and control that the waterlogged track made little difference to his speed and he won; he was on his way.

His record from then on was testimony to that extraordinary will to win: he came second in the next three races in the Townsend Thorensen Championship, then he won the opening race in the RAC Championship at Oulton Park; three more victories followed, followed by a second place, then he won every other race, save for one slip where he finished fourth, before the final race in the RAC Championship at Snetterton on 9 August which he won, taking the title. He also won the final in the Townsend Thorensen Championship at Donington Park, taking that title too, and in the pits Liliane and his parents, who had come over for the race, went wild with excitement.

Out of the eighteen races he had contested he had won twelve, with two pole positions and ten fastest laps; he also won the Formula Ford title in Brazil. It was a record which should have brought him advancement, but it brought him only confusion in himself. Liliane was not suited to the nomadic life of a racing wife with a base in rural Norfolk, keeping house

*Birth of a
Champion:
in August 1981,
Ayrton Senna
clinched two
premier Formula
Ford 1600
championships,
the Townsend
Thorensen and
the RAC.*

herself in a rented bungalow. She was used to servants, sun and a good life. He was pursuing what he wanted to do, but she was not, and their marriage was not turning out to be what either wanted. His father had said he would support him financially for a year and that time was now up and Milton da Silva was pressing Ayrton to give up motor racing and to enter the family business. But the lure of racing was even more powerful now on the back of his incredible success.

Driving in the lower formulas was not a job, it was a very expensive hobby. The only way to make it pay was to get sponsorship, and all the young Brazilian drivers tried hard to get sponsorship in Brazil which, despite his success, he could not find. Part of the problem was that he was not alone in coming to Europe from Brazil to get into the sport. Two of the new wave of Brazilian drivers were ahead of him, already driving in Formula Three, and both were winning. Roberto Moreno had made a great success of his Formula Three season, finishing in the points in sixteen out of twenty races, winning three of them and finishing third in the Marlboro Formula Three Championship. This Championship was the acknowledged last stop before being offered a Formula One drive. Raul Boesel was also doing well in Formula Three and the pair were getting interest from the press back home, and the sponsorship. Formula Ford 1600 did not have the profile of Formula Three and with the Brazilian economy not being in the best of shape, heading for hyper-inflation, Senna had little success.

At the top of the heap in getting sponsorship was Nelson Piquet who had stolen the headlines in 1981 as he steadily advanced towards the world title to great acclaim at home in Brazil, becoming the second Brazilian to become World Champion. Nelson Piquet,

Young Love:
Ayrton Senna da
Silva celebrating
his first
triumphant
season in
England with
his wife, Liliane;
they separated
after a year.

the son a former Brazilian Minister of Health, had a reputation as something of a playboy. He was an uncharismatic driver, never doing more than enough to carefully accumulate the points, not one of the red-blooded types. But that was a small detail alongside the fact that he had won races, that was what counted when it came to sponsorship.

Brazil was also going through a bout of inflation which would ultimately lead to political upheaval in 1985, and Piquet's success came just as Emerson Fittipaldi's dream of a Brazilian-based Formula One team had come to an embarrassing halt. After two World Championships, Fittipaldi had left McLaren to form Copersucar, an all Brazilian team backed with huge sums by the country's sugar corporation. The idea had been patriotic, and it was run by Emerson's brother Wilson. It had been in business for six years and had very little to show for the sponsorship which had been poured in.

To Ayrton Senna, the world seemed stacked against him. He had done everything, but he was not getting the support he wanted. Others had squeezed him out of the honey pot of sponsorship and he did not like it. In October, having won the two Formula Ford 1600 Championships, he announced his retirement. Success and talent counted for little he felt, and his comment to the press at the end of the season revealed his frustration and disillusion with the sport of motor racing; it also revealed his sense of himself as the point around which the world should revolve: 'In racing talent is not important; a bad driver with money can get a good team, but a good driver with little money can only get a bad team.'

Back in Sao Paulo he went to work for his father managing a building supplies business.

CHAPTER THREE

APPRENTICESHIP

Four months in the building business was enough. Not even a regular job, the comfort of being with his family again and of being back in his beloved Brazil could compensate for missing the opportunity to compete, and to win. At 21, Ayrton Senna da Silva had tasted the thrill of winning races and two championships, and he missed it. He would often go to see his friend Mauricio Gugelmin racing karts in Brazil, and seeing him winning was too much, there was nothing less than a burning desire to get back into motor racing.

The pull of England was easier, if not greater, because after a year of marriage he and Liliane had decided to separate. The year in Norfolk had been a happy time for both of them, but Liliane was not suited to life in the English countryside, especially in winter, and they decided they were not suited to each other. He had found the perfect outlet for his quiet energies and was drawn further and further into doing what he loved doing, which was to win, and that increasingly took over his life. She had little to do other than follow him, and she was used to a more glamorous lifestyle which was not to be found in lower formula motor racing in Britain.

His knack of getting what he wanted had not deserted him. After much discussion inside the family, his father left him to decide between business and racing. Unsurprisingly, he chose racing and when he did Milton da Silva agreed to provide some of the money, though he also managed to get sponsorship from a Brazilian bank, Banerj.

Instead of windy Snetterton in Norfolk, this time he went to Donington Park in Derbyshire, Britain's first real road racing circuit and the scene of British Grands Prix in the 1930s. Donington was the home of

Silverstone, in the British Formula Ford 2000 Championship: Ayrton Senna in the Rushen Green RF82-Ford; next on the grid is his great rival in 1982, Calvin Fish.

the Rushen Green Formula Ford 2000 team run by Dennis Rushen. He had Van Diemen cars produced by Ralph Firmin, whose 1.6 litre cars Senna had raced in 1981, and it was Firmin who had stayed in touch on the phone from Britain during the winter, encouraging him to return to racing.

Senna arrived from Brazil in February, entering the Pace Petroleum Championship and in the European 2000 Championship. He drove in his first race at Brands Hatch on 7 March. He took pole position and won by 14 seconds, taking fastest lap too. The statistics of the next few weeks show just why Firmin had been right, from the point of view of racing, to urge him to keep trying: on 27 March he took pole, fastest lap and won at Oulton Park, beating the much fancied British driver, Calvin Fish, by 10 seconds; the next day he took pole, fastest lap and won at Silverstone; repeating the performance at Donington on 4 April; and a week later at Snetterton he did the same, even though he had lost his front brakes. The next day it was back to Silverstone for pole, fastest lap and another win.

With that level of performance it was not long before the Formula One teams began to show an interest. Alex Hawkridge of Toleman and Ron Dennis of McLaren approached him indicating that they might sponsor him through a season in Formula Three which, under new rules being introduced at the time, was a requirement for getting a Formula One licence. Senna's reaction was not the one they expected, he kept talking but was reluctant to conclude a deal. He clearly understood that he was now an interesting proposition for Formula One, a very different situation from the previous year. He also thought he needed more experience in the lower formulas where engine power, tyres and many other variables in the cars were

pretty much the same, the difference being the driver. In Formula One, the difference in the performance of the cars is huge, and highly dependent on the degree of financial support the team gets. He wanted to be World Champion and he did not want to attach himself to a contract which gave others power of decision over him: he wanted to stay as free an agent as possible; he wanted to feel right about moving to Formula One himself, having weighed the possibilities and the advantages of the particular teams; and he wanted to make his own decisions. He was fortunate, he could

afford to do so. Most young drivers in his position would have jumped at the chance of sponsorship by a Formula One team, and it was a very confident move for a young man, revealing again that streak of determination to do business on his own terms.

He was much more confident in 1982, which may in part have been due to living with Mauricio Gugelmin who, in addition to karting, had won the Brazilian Formula Ford 1600 Championship in Brazil in 1981. He had followed Senna to Britain, and was based at Snetterton with his wife, Stella. For Senna their

Jyllandsring, Denmark, 22 August 1982: Ayrton Senna clinching the European 2000 series; of the nine races he won six and took eight pole positions.

home was a little island of Brazil that was many miles away from home; he had Brazilians to talk to and Stella to mother him.

Not all Brazilians were as friendly. At Zolder in Belgium on 9 May he was racing in a European 2000 race. He took pole position, but had to retire with an engine fault. It was held on the same weekend as the Belgian Grand Prix in which Gilles Villeneuve was killed in practice. All the young Formula Ford 2000 drivers had ambitions to make it into Formula One, where the drivers were the gods and Senna sought out

Nelson Piquet, the reigning World Champion and a fellow Brazilian. Senna found him, but Piquet made it plain he wanted nothing to do with him, and Senna, a man of great selfishness himself, but a very courteous one nevertheless, was taken aback and upset.

On 30 May at Oulton Park, Calvin Fish was leading Senna and Kenny Andrews in a pack at the front of a race, the cars close together at 125 mph. Suddenly Senna's rear right tyre exploded, and in an instant he was going sideways round the corner. His extraordinary instincts took over and with three wheels only he managed to get the car pointing down the circuit again, completing two more corners before waving Andrews past.

Encouraged by his victory at Oulton Park, and with a new car too, Calvin Fish took pole position at Brands Hatch the following day. Senna, however, firmly took the lead on the first lap and fought off the challenge from Fish to win by 2 seconds, scoring the fastest lap too. A week later, he won at Mallory Park, also taking fastest lap. At Snetterton on 1 August, he was leading from Fish again, when on Lap 6 Fish pulled out on a long straight to overtake. The two cars were alongside each other, when Senna started weaving across the circuit, pushing Fish towards the grass, trying to intimidate him into lifting off and getting back behind. Fish held hard, but Senna left him no room and Fish was forced on to the grass, bouncing into the air as he did so. Fish retired and Senna went on to win but Fish made an official complaint and Senna was fined by the RAC, though he kept his points in the Championship. Relations with Fish inevitably cooled, but that mattered little to Senna.

It was Senna versus Fish that season, in both Championships. At Zandvoort, in round five of the

European 2000, Senna missed the first practice session because of a clutch problem leaving him only one session in which to learn the circuit. He learned it well, taking pole position and winning his first race in Europe. Fish came second after a tremendous battle for second place with Cor Euser, putting him just 2 points behind Senna for the European title.

In June, Senna went to a Formula Three test day on the club circuit at Silverstone. His father was over from Brazil to visit him and came to watch. He had been approached by Eddie Jordan who had just started his team and was looking for promising young drivers. Senna did thirty-eight laps in all, the best in 54.03 seconds, an astonishing time for a first drive in what was a completely new car for him. Compared with 54.4 seconds, the best time at the previous race meeting on the club circuit on Whit Sunday, it made him all the more attractive as a Formula Three prospect. Jordan and Ron Dennis of McLaren continued to discuss sponsoring him for a season, but his cautious attitude about committing himself was evident and he said after the race that he wanted to try out other Formula Three cars before signing up.

He won at Hockenheim, taking pole and fastest lap, then repeated the performance in Austria at the Ostreichring. Calvin Fish was still only just behind him in the Championship and it looked likely that they would settle the Euroseries at the Jyllandsring in Denmark. Senna took pole position, but Fish was back in sixth place on the grid. Fish had a good start and managed to get into second place behind Senna. But Senna was on top form, breaking the Formula Ford 2000 lap record for the circuit at 46.04 seconds, then winning the race and taking the European title by 2.5 seconds from Fish. As he appeared on the podium his eyes were red from crying.

On 30 August at Thruxton, Fish took pole position by 0.3 seconds from Senna, then led the race with Senna chasing hard. On Lap 4, Senna's car developed problems which prevented him from making a bid for the lead until Lap 13 when he overtook Fish, nursing his car which had oil smoke pouring from the exhaust. He won, smashing the lap record too.

Of the twenty-eight races he entered in Formula Ford 2000 in 1982, Ayrton Senna won twenty-two, retired four times with technical problems, and came second twice, taking the EFDA Euroseries and in Britain, the Pace Petroleum Championships.

To round off the Formula Three season in style, there was a televised non-championship race at Thruxton, a showcase for the best of the drivers knocking on the door from the lower formulas. Senna was driving for Dick Bennetts' Formula Three West Surrey Racing team, and he caused what was becoming an anticipated sensation during testing two weeks before the race, lapping Thruxton faster than anybody else at the session, first by 0.75 seconds, then by 0.85 seconds. Then he broke the lap record by 0.2 seconds, finishing up in his customary pole position with a lap time of 1 minute 13.34 seconds, 0.6 of a second faster than one of the strongest regular Formula Three drivers at the time, Martin Brundle, who had taken pole position at Thruxton just two weeks before. Calvin Fish was also at the test, finishing a full second behind Senna.

Reports of the race are brief. He made a perfect start, led all the way, stretching his lead to 13 seconds over 15 laps, to win his first race in a Formula Three car. *Autosport* magazine's report was prophetic: 'Here is a World Champion in the making, for sure.'

Close encounter: in the Formula Three race at Oulton Park on August 6 1983, the rivalry between Ayrton Senna and Martin Brundle reached a peak when they touched wheels putting them both out of the race.

After a winter in Brazil he was back for the twenty-race Marlboro British Formula Three Championship in March 1983, the last stop before moving up to Formula One. He could have had the pick of the teams but he chose West Surrey with whom he had won his debut race at Thruxton. He got on well with Dick Bennetts, and also felt that this team represented his best prospect of winning the title. Bennetts had taken Stefan Johannson to the Formula Three Championship in 1980, Jonathan Palmer in 1981, and in 1982 they had taken Enrique Mansilla, an Argentinian, to second place. Senna had raced against Mansilla, and in his view, he had not performed as well as he might in West Surrey's cars. He felt that a team which could get those results with Mansilla was a team which knew how to prepare its cars.

With his record in Formula Ford 1600 and Formula Ford 2000, Senna was tipped to be the top man in Formula Three in 1983. This irked Martin Brundle, the great British Formula Three hope, who had had a strong year in 1982 and was now driving for Eddie Jordan. Senna had been given a huge boost by winning the televised Formula Three event in 1983, but he hadn't even driven in a Championship race yet: it seemed premature to put Senna on such a pedestal. There was little love lost between Senna and Jordan either. Jordan had given him his first taste of Formula Three but Senna had chosen to go to West Surrey. There was nothing wrong with that, but Senna had a way of distancing himself from other people on the circuit, remaining aloof, barely exchanging any words with his closest rivals when they met at circuits, and keeping himself apart from the crowd. This seemingly arrogant stance did not endear him to many people, and as the season opened there was an attitude towards

The taste of victory, 22 August 1982; Ayrton Senna at Jyllandsring after winning his first international championship, the European Formula Ford 2000.

him, an unspoken question hanging in the air: 'Who does this guy think he is?'.

They soon found out. Up to 1982, he had been known by his full name, Ayrton Senna da Silva, but before the start of the 1983 season he let it be known to the press that he wanted to be known simply as Ayrton Senna.

Ayrton Senna could only qualify second fastest for the first race at Silverstone, behind the Scottish driver David Leslie. Brundle was in fourth place on the grid, just in front of Senna's old sparring partner from Formula Ford 2000, Calvin Fish. On the first corner they found out that Senna had lost none of his edge. Leslie made a good start and took the line going into the first corner, but Senna took an outside line and drove the long way round into the lead. Brundle moved up to second place, but over twenty laps Senna stretched his lead to 7 seconds; Brundle was second.

As the season progressed he showed his detractors why they were right to treat him differently. He took pole, fastest lap and won at Silverstone in a torrential storm, then won again at Thruxton while suffering from a bout of flu. He went on winning despite the usual motor racing hitches and his fair share of technical problems including underpowered engines and, on one occasion at Silverstone, a faulty fire extinguisher in the engine compartment which went off unprompted. Even Brundle had to marvel at the sheer cheek and nerve of his driving; Senna passed him on the outside more than once.

With such progress, Bennetts lavished all the team's attention on Senna. It was exactly what he wanted, but it was not purely selfish, his argument was that it worked for the team, too, since he paid back their investment with a good dividend. It was a

performance which created its own virtuous circle: he had won every race, and that in itself intimidated the opposition – his studied aloofness around the pits and his reputation for an almost obsessive level of attention to detail all added to the invincible aura, just as Senna intended it to. It was all part of his racing persona. Always being first summed up his whole approach to racing, starting in qualifying, where he was always at his most competitive and never liked to be anywhere except on pole. In the first few seconds of a race he would go for the lead straight away where he demonstrated his feeling that he had a right to be there, putting distance between him and the opposition, making them follow, controlling the race from the front. His aggressive approach made other drivers that little bit more wary of him, giving him a status both on and off the circuit, and it paid off handsomely: he won the first nine races of the season, beating the record of eight, set by Nelson Piquet in 1978.

In the nine races Senna had won, Martin Brundle had been second eight times and third once. He was disappointed, but refused to be intimidated. At Silverstone on 12 May he resolved to match Senna's forceful approach and get out in front himself. In the first round of the European Championship he went for the fastest set-up he could and snatched pole position, then went into the lead. Senna was using three different types of tyre, a policy which failed, and after two laps he was having handling problems, spinning off on Lap 6 to rejoin in ninth place. Brundle's confident approach was working; Senna was under pressure, he was behind and he did not like it. He used every bit of skill to catch up, and in doing so he made a mistake at the chicane on Lap 8, spinning off and flying backwards into the catch fencing. He was out of the race, to the great satisfaction of the Jordan team as Brundle took his first race of the season.

The spell had been broken and suddenly Formula Three came alive. At Cadwell Park, Senna took pole position, but it was as if he felt he was still under pressure. He had to have more than pole position, and the little demon in him which said 'go faster, always do better, never be satisfied' took over. With pole position in the bag, he smashed Enrique Mansilla's year-old lap record. Then, with just 2 minutes of qualifying time left, he pushed it too far, straying just wide on to the grass coming out of a right-hand corner. He ran out of road and crashed heavily into a marshal's dugout, injuring the marshal.

Ayrton Senna at Donington for the fourth round of the British Formula Three Championship; he had won the previous three and went on to win nine in succession.

Silverstone, 31 May 1983: Ayrton Senna's ninth successive victory in the British Formula Three Championship; Martin Brundle (right) had been second eight times.

The car was smashed and since there was no spare he was out of the race; Brundle won.

Senna's progress had been checked. After nine straight wins, Brundle had shown that Senna was subject to pressure, that he was not invincible and that there was a way to beat him. Brundle was the only driver in a position to do it and their rivalry became highly personal – a needle match – and the clash of personalities, as well as the close racing, began to draw huge crowds, with more time being devoted to Formula Three on television.

The next race was at Snetterton, and everybody expected some kind of showdown. Senna could only qualify fourth, behind Johnny Dumfries, Brundle and an American driver, David Jones. The problem was with his car, it was down on power. Dumfries later crashed in qualifying and did not start. Brundle, who effectively had pole, took the lead. Senna got ahead of

Jones at the start and set out after Brundle. But the man who was by now his nemesis, was pulling away. By Lap 8, Senna was pulling back Brundle's lead and the crowd was buzzing with delight. He steadily advanced, and halfway round Lap 23 he challenged Brundle. Brundle was on the left of the track, off the racing line and Senna was challenging on his left, expecting Brundle to give way. But Brundle stayed put, and first one of Senna's wheels, then another, went on to the grass. The cars came closer and closer together, neither giving way. Then the wheels touched and Senna was flung back, spinning right across the track into the Armco barrier on the other side. Brundle went on to win his third race, while Senna failed to finish for the third time. Afterwards Senna lodged a complaint against Brundle, but to no avail, leaving him with 89 points in the Championship to Brundle's 73.

Senna driving West Surrey Racing's Formula Three Ralt RT3-Toyota for the cameras at Donington on 27 March 1983; he took pole, fastest lap and won the race.

The pair were on the front row of the grid together at Silverstone for the next race on 16 July, Senna this time on pole, Brundle just 0.4 seconds slower. The race was in support of the British Grand Prix and all the Formula One managers were there looking over the new talent. This time Senna's team had found the power and he was out in front by the first corner, back into his old routine. In a post-race interview, he ended with the comment 'we are back to normal.'

Not quite. Brundle was still fighting, his natural talent and competitiveness brought out by the heightened rivalry. A week later they were alongside each other on the grid at Donington on 24 July. Senna was on pole, with a time of 1 second under his own lap record, but again it was Brundle who made the storming start, reaching Redgate corner on the racing line before Senna could do anything about it, and

opening out a slight lead on the first lap. Senna chased all the way, and in the closing laps he did everything he could to catch up, cutting across kerbs, going on to the grass, but the gap was stubbornly difficult to reduce. Brundle was in charge, but the spectators got their money's worth, the winning margin was just over half a second.

The first offer of a test drive for Formula One came from Frank Williams at Donington later that week. Senna had been to ask Williams' advice on how to cope with the various teams who were offering him a drive in return for a long-term commitment. Williams had no room in his own team for 1984 – he had Keke Rosberg, who had won the 1982 Drivers' Championship for Williams, and he had taken on Jacques Laffite from Ligier – but he wanted to give a helping hand to what was clearly a driver of the future, 'a long-term investment' as he put it.

It was a moment for which Senna had been planning and dreaming for many years, all his young life in many ways, but as he sat in the Williams he was unfazed by it. The driving position was quite uncomfortable – he was using a seat moulded to the shape of the smaller Laffite – but he put in some respectable times during the eighty-three laps and returned the car in one piece. As the test ended, Williams confirmed that it did not mean that Senna would be joining him but he suggested that Bernard Ecclestone of Brabham could be interested.

Meanwhile back in Formula Three, in the fifthteenth race of the Championship on 6 August at Oulton Park, Brundle was faster in qualifying, taking pole position by 0.3 of a second from Senna. Brundle took the lead and stayed there for most of the race, with Senna around a car's length behind until Lap 29.

Donington,
19 July 1983;
Ayrton Senna's
first Formula One
test drive;
Frank Williams
was impressed
how quickly he
mastered the
Williams FW08C.

Brundle was having a braking problem which meant he had to brake fractionally earlier on the corners than he would have chosen to. This gave Senna a tiny opening each time they went into a corner, and he decided that there was a gap he could go through on the inside at Fosters. He tried, came into contact with Brundle's rear wheel which pitched him right on top of Brundle's car, putting them both out and giving Calvin Fish his first Formula Three victory. Senna was fined by the RAC and his licence was endorsed.

Senna won his eleventh victory at Silverstone, giving him 116 points to Brundle's 94. This meant that at the next race at Oulton in early September, Senna only needed to come second to win the Championship. Brundle took the lead with Senna just behind and had he stayed there he would have won the title. Senna just had to win though, and even with the Championship apparently his, he went for it, trying to take Brundle on the outside. He crashed and retired.

A race later at Thruxton, Senna took pole position but retired with mechanical problems; Brundle won. Suddenly it was Senna's 116 points to Brundle's 113, and a week later at Silverstone, Brundle beat him into second place to lead the Championship by a single point. This injected a new excitement into their battle and there were great expectations for the denouement of the Championship in the last race at Thruxton on 23 October. They were misplaced. It was a tame end to the Championship, largely because Senna had left nothing to chance in preparing his car, even driving to Italy with his racing engine in his boot to have it rebuilt and tuned by Novamotor, the best engine tuners in the business. Brundle's car was not at its best; Senna took pole and won a relatively easy twelfth victory and with it the British Formula Three Championship.

Test drive debrief with Frank Williams: one of the Senna's great gifts was his ability to recall every last detail of a drive for later discussion and analysis.

Donington, 1983: Ayrton Senna celebrating his fourth successive victory in the British Formla Three Championship for West Surrey Racing.

Man on the move: Ayrton Senna graduated to Formula One at the age of 23 having spent a year in each of the lower formulas, winning the Championship in all three.

The following month, Senna was halfway round the world in Macau, a Portuguese possession on the coast of China, for the Formula Three Macau Grand Prix. He won. Negotiations with the Formula One teams now started in earnest and as part of them there were more test drives. McLaren tested Ayrton Senna, Martin Brundle and Stefan Bellof at Silverstone. Senna was fastest, with a lap of 1 minute 13.9 seconds, faster than McLaren's top driver, Niki Lauda, had done in qualifying for the British Grand Prix. But, McLaren

had Niki Lauda and had just signed Alain Prost from Renault so there was no room for a new driver in the team; it was another long-term investment by Ron Dennis.

Toleman was next and they did have space: their star driver, Derek Warwick, had gone to Renault. Senna did seventy-two laps of Silverstone, getting the time down to 1 minute 11.54 seconds, a second better than Warwick's time in qualifying for the British Grand Prix. He did it despite gear selection problems, and without them he was confident that he could have got under 1 minute 11 seconds.

Lastly, came Brabham. Bernard Ecclestone did have space, but he was having a tussle with his main sponsors, the Italian firm, Parmalat, about filling the No. 2 spot. Their top driver, Nelson Piquet had just won the World Championship and he was secure, but Parmalat wanted an Italian driver as No. 2. Brabham tried out new drivers at the Paul Ricard circuit in France where Piquet was getting to grips with the new BT52B. Ecclestone brought along four new drivers: Mauro Baldi and Pierluigi Martini from Italy, Robert Guerro from Colombia, and Ayrton Senna. Piquet put up a time of 1 minute 5.9 seconds, Senna and Baldi were only 2 seconds slower at 1 minute 7.9 seconds, with Guerro and Martini at 1 minute 8.6 seconds. Ecclestone wanted Senna.

Senna wanted to go to Brabham, but there was a problem: Nelson Piquet did not want Senna in the same team. Senna had a reputation as somebody who would never be No. 2, who would be going for the Championship both off and on the track, demanding the attention which would detract from the Champion. Between them, Piquet and Parmalat ensured that Senna would not be coming to Brabham.

Ayrton Senna was approached by several Formula One teams during this triumphant year in Formula Three, finally settling for Toleman.

CHAPTER FOUR

MUSICAL CHAIRS

Formula One is about winning and nothing else. It is about difficult choices and ruthless decisions. The team with the best driver does not always win, not unless he has the right car, the right engine, the right tyres, the latest aerodynamics, enough money, and the best support from the rest of the team. A brilliant driver will make up for small deficiencies in the car, but a big difference in power or handling will always show, no matter how talented the man behind the wheel. As the sponsors' money ebbs and flows through the system, so the performance of the cars, and the team which supports them, will rise and fall. Halfway through each season, a game of 'musical chairs' starts, as team managers look around for the best talent, then reconcile this choice with sponsors' needs and with the other driver in the team. It starts at the top, as national undercurrents, the commercial interests of sponsors, the talents of the drivers, the possibility of personality clashes and the unseen hand of pure economics, play their parts.

Getting the best drive is the objective of the drivers. Sometimes the move is obvious and quite easy, but sometimes the struggle for the right seat can go on to the end of the year before the final deals are done. Finding a clear path through the politics is important for a young driver who needs to start the virtuous circle of winning, getting more sponsorship, driving better cars, winning.

Promising careers can be ruined, if, when the music stops, a driver is without a drive. It is very difficult to improve after a season spent on the back of the grid and only the most exceptional drivers make it. Most go into a downward spiral to the less competitive teams, where they win less, have more work to do, fail to finish races, lose.

Winning the Formula Three Championship had made Ayrton Senna a hot property, and he expected to start near the top, but the top teams — Williams, Brabham and McLaren — either had no vacancies or he was vetoed by another driver. Toleman was a small team founded on the back of Ted Toleman's haulage business. Derek Warwick had been with them since 1980, but after three seasons he went to Renault in the hope of improving his own chances of becoming World Champion. Senna fitted Toleman's needs perfectly: he was obviously good, and Alex Hawkridge, the team manager, could not afford one of the stars. Essentially the choice was between Ayrton Senna and Martin Brundle, who had also had a test drive with Tyrell.

Peter Warr of Lotus was also interested in Senna after they made contact at the European Grand Prix at Brands Hatch in 1982, but Lotus, which had once been one of the top teams, was in something of a decline following the death of Colin Chapman in 1982. Chapman had a brilliant eye for new drivers, and he had picked the team's two drivers, Elio de Angelis and Nigel Mansell, before his death. De Angelis had driven some good races for Lotus, but had only won one Grand Prix. Mansell, who had taken Chapman's death very badly, had yet to win one, though he had put Lotus on the second row of the grid at the British Grand Prix. He was also very popular with the British fans, an important point with Lotus' sponsors, John Player. Warr decided to stick with his existing drivers, but he and Senna stayed in touch.

It was Senna's first experience of musical chairs at the top, but he had prepared himself for it. He saw much of the manoeuvring as very personal, a sign that the establishment of Formula One was stacked against him. Bernard Ecclestone, who had pushed as hard as

Portugese Grand Prix, Estoril, 21 October 1984: Ayrton Senna's last race for Toleman-Hart; he finished third.

possible to sign him for Brabham, finally admitted defeat at the hands of Parmalat and Nelson Piquet and told Senna in early December 1983 that it was no good. Senna, who had been keeping the offer from Toleman open until he knew the score at Brabham, then signed a three-year contract with them, something of a coup for Toleman considering the level of interest in him; Toleman's second driver was the Venezuelan, Johnny Cecotto. Brundle signed for Tyrell, and Ecclestone brought in the Italian driver, Teo Fabi, who had had mixed fortunes in Formula One before departing for Indycar racing; he was still committed to the American series, but agreed to drive in Grands Prix when he could.

Toleman was a young team and they did not have the best of everything. Their new car was not ready for the 1984 season, so Senna started his career in the previous year's car, the TG183. Nor did they have the most competitive tyres. They used Pirellis, while most of the top teams were supplied by the leading racing-tyre maker, Goodyear, from America, or the French company, Michelin.

But he had made it to Formula One and, by a twist of good fortune, the first race was the Brazilian Grand Prix in Rio. It was a very proud moment for him, and his entire family turned out to watch. His parents, reconciled to his career as a racing driver, had become great supporters, coming over to Britain to see him race whenever possible, and he was immensely proud to be racing in front of them, particularly on their home ground. Senna qualified eighth on the grid, but in the race he had problems with turbo boost pressure and had to retire. Martin Brundle, his old sparring partner from Formula Three was fifth for Tyrell, though he was later disqualified. It was a memorable

day for Senna, but to drop out in front of his family and his countrymen had its miserable side too.

Senna wanted to swap from Pirellis to better tyres, and Toleman eventually struck a deal to use Michelin's previous year's tyres, the 1984 editions being reserved for their main customers, Renault, Brabham and McLaren. The deal provided for Toleman to continue on Pirellis for the San Marino Grand Prix, rather than embarrass Pirelli on its home ground in Italy, and for the first and only time in his career Ayrton Senna did not qualify for a race. Since he was getting what he wanted in the long run, more competitive tyres for the French Grand Prix at Dijon, he was content to wait. With four Grands Prix under his belt, he was not doing as well as he would have liked: he had failed to qualify once; retired once; come sixth; only to be disqualified for being two laps behind in Belgium; and come sixth in South Africa.

There was a welcome break from Formula One for a celebrity race to mark the opening of the new Nurburgring in Germany, a circuit resonant with history and the great days of German supremacy in motor racing in the 1930s with Auto Union and Mercedes. Mercedes chose the circuit to launch its new 190E saloon car, organizing a galaxy of former World Champions and current racing drivers to drive them: Stirling Moss, Jack Brabham, Carlos Reutemann, James Hunt, Hans Herrman, Phil Hill, John Surtees, Denny Hulme, Alain Prost and John Watson, amongst others, all of whom had made their livelihoods out of being competitive on the race track. It was partly fun, but Senna wanted to show the world what he could do, and it was a perfect opportunity. He won by 2.5 seconds from double World Champion Niki Lauda.

It was a great boost to his spirits as he returned to prepare for the French Grand Prix, his will to win recharged by the taste of victory. His single-mindedness, and his demanding nature were already having their effect inside Toleman and when preparing for a race, he worked tirelessly himself, testing, debriefing and expecting others to share the long hours. In doing so he steadily hijacked the team's resources in support of him, and Johnny Cecotto, who had been in Formula One a year longer than Senna, was slowly edged out. Senna put him in the shade, both on the track and inside the team. For the French Grand Prix, Senna got the new TG184 car, while Cecotto had to continue with the TG183: both retired with turbo problems.

His sixth Grand Prix, and the social high point of the season, was at Monaco. Prost showed why McLaren had hired him by putting the TAG-Porsche powered MP4/2 in pole position with 1 minute 22.661 seconds, but the sensation of qualifying was Nigel Mansell who put Lotus second on the grid with 1 minute 22.752 seconds. The World Champion, Nelson Piquet, was back in ninth place, and Senna qualified thirteenth with 1 minute 25.009 seconds.

Race day was heavily overcast and everybody knew it was going to rain. Michelin only had their latest stock of wet weather tyres, so they had to let Toleman have them otherwise they would have been unable to race, which suited Senna as much as the weather. Prost went into the lead, followed by Mansell, and Lauda moved up to third place. By the end of the first lap, Piquet and Senna had swapped places, Senna up to ninth, while Piquet slipped to thirteenth.

The wet was a great leveller and by Lap 7 Senna had gained two more places before Michele Alboreto spun off putting him sixth. He sensed that he could achieve something and pushed a little too hard and a little too close to the kerb in the chicane on Lap 11, getting the Toleman airborne. On the next lap he moved up to fifth when Keke Rosberg's Williams started misfiring and he was out. Teo Fabi spun on the same lap, finishing up in the middle of the track, and when Prost came up on the stationary car suddenly, he only narrowly missed it, striking one of the marshals who was trying to move it a glancing blow. Prost was thrown by the incident and he slowed. This gave Mansell just the chance he had been looking for, and he was through into the lead, the first time he had ever been at the front in a Grand Prix.

Prost did not like the wet, and once ahead, Mansell put on the pressure, pulling away at around 2 seconds a lap. Like Senna he was a racer, a winner, and like Senna

Nurbergring, Germany, 12 May 1984: Ayrton Senna pressing Niki Lauda in identical Mercedes 190Es during the inaugural race at the circuit; Senna won against nine former World Champions.

he sometimes tried too hard: he spun on a slippery piece of road marking, finishing up in the Armco barrier. Lauda then made a small error on Lap 18 and spun off too, putting Senna in second place. The rain got heavier and heavier, and as it did, so Senna moved up on Prost. On Lap 20 the gap between the two was 33.8 seconds; eleven laps later, as they went into Lap 31, it was down to 7.4 seconds. Prost had been indicating for some time that he was fed up with the wet, and he was shaking his fist each time he passed the start/finish line. On Lap 31 he got his way. The Clerk of the Course, Jackie Ickx, decided that enough was enough and stopped the race. Prost slowed and Senna caught up quickly, surging past as they crossed the line. Senna thought he had won, but sadly for him, the final positions are those on the lap where the red flag went out, putting him second.

The World Championship erupted in a fit of conflicting interests. Toleman and Senna were outraged. Just as they were about to make the breakthrough which would have established them among the top teams, it was whipped away from them by officials interpreting the rules. Had the race lasted a few more laps there was every likelihood that Senna would have taken Prost in the Frenchman's back yard, and in the most prestigious race of the year. Inevitably, there were suggestions of a French conspiracy – giving Prost the race just as Senna was getting too close for comfort. Senna was angry, but he showed little of his emotions in public, accepting his disappointment stoically. He had been out there and in eleven laps he had learned something and he had shown what he could do in a second rank car. He had given the establishment a nasty fright: they had seen that given the right circumstances, he could gain on Prost in a

top rank car. He was the driver who, in conditions when nobody could see the car in front and had to listen for the sound of its engine, had driven the fastest lap; his time would come.

Most reports of the race invoked history to describe Senna's drive, awarding him the title 'Regenmeister', which had first been bestowed on Rudolf Caracciola, the great Mercedes driver, at Monaco in 1936. Caracciola, one of the greatest drivers in the history of the sport had shown the same quality of being able to drive in bad weather without dropping his speed dramatically.

The US round in the Championship included two Grands Prix in 1984, in Dallas and Detroit. In Dallas, after the first round of qualifying, there was a sports car race which had reduced parts of the surface to rubble, and when it came to the second qualifying session, the Toleman manager, Peter Gethin, decided that since it was highly unlikely that anybody would improve their times, it was not worth going out. Senna disagreed; he wanted to go out and try, and he reacted to Gethin's instructions with a display of truculence and emotion. He was not going to be told what to do, he wanted to do things his way, so he ignored Gethin and went out. When he came back they had an almighty row. He stood up for himself, but inside he was hurting and humiliated and there was no going back for him: the Toleman management had got it wrong and for him the relationship deteriorated.

He was coming to the conclusion that Toleman, however dedicated it was, and it was, simply did not have the resources or the management to make him World Champion, and certainly not in the time-scale he had set himself. The high point of the team's history had been his second place at Monaco, and that was not

New kid on the block: Ayrton Senna, aged 24, at the US Grand Prix in Dallas, Texas, in his first season in Formula One; he retired with a broken driveshaft.

good enough for him. Then, to add to the team's problems, Michelin announced that it was pulling out of racing at the end of the season. This left them without tyres again, putting Senna's hopes of winning back still further.

By the time the musical chairs for the 1985 season started in July, Senna had made up his mind that he would change teams. He had signed a three-year contract with Toleman, but under it he could buy himself out, though he was obliged to let them know if he was in negotiation with another team. He didn't. Instead, he renewed his contacts with Peter Warr at Lotus and they started negotiations.

Senna came third for Toleman at the British Grand Prix; Johnny Cecotto was badly injured in a crash, marking the end of his career. At Hockenheim, for the German race, Senna's rear aerofoil failed at around 200 mph on the fourth Lap when he was lying fifth. He started spinning, conscious only that if he could somehow make the rear of the car hit the barrier first he would be safe. That is what happened, and he walked away unscathed. After that experience, for the first time, he let it be known that he believed he had been saved by the intervention of God.

Lotus and their sponsors, John Player, were keen to announce that Senna was going to drive for them in 1985 at the Dutch Grand Prix at Zandvoort on 26 August, and they released a press notice to that effect. It was the first that Toleman had heard of the negotiations and when they confronted Senna, he confirmed that he had an agreement, but that he had not agreed to let the news come out that way. He was unhappy at the way that it happened, but he learned another lesson about the way things happen at the top of Formula One. So did Nigel Mansell, who had been

having a poor season with Lotus, and who heard the same day that he was to be replaced by Senna.

The effect on Toleman was shattering. They had lost their top driver, they had no tyre contract, having burnt their boats with Pirelli, and now they looked a pretty unlikely outfit to attract any prospective sponsor. Senna was largely indifferent to their plight: the Toleman management had humiliated him, however mildly, and now he had humiliated them. Toleman decided that they could not just let it pass and to get back at him they chose the only way it would hurt, by stopping him driving. Before the Italian Grand Prix at Monza, they signed Stefan Johannson, who was without a drive because Tyrell had been disqualified from the whole season's results following a breach of the rules. There were still two cars, following Cecotto's departure, but Senna was told he would not be driving. He did not believe them at first, but they stuck to their guns, and he had to sit it out; Johansson came fourth.

Toleman reinstated Senna for the Portugese Grand Prix which promised to be a hard fought race since the World Championship was still undecided.

The battle was between the two McLaren drivers, Niki Lauda and Alain Prost and Lauda needed only second place to take the title, even if Prost won. For most of the race Lauda was third, behind Mansell and Prost, with Senna fourth. But Mansell spun off, Lauda came second, taking the Championship, and Senna came third, giving him a welcome place on the podium as Lauda celebrated victory. That year, Senna finished equal ninth with Nigel Mansell in the World Championship with 13 points.

Senna's new contract with Lotus was for two years officially, and he was named as 'joint No.1' driver with Elio de Angelis. Mansell went to drive for Williams as a replacement for Jacques Laffite

Career move 1985: Ayrton Senna with Elio de Angelis and the Lotus-Renault 97T; he replaced Nigel Mansell who had been with the team for five years.

who had gone back to Ligier. Williams had offered the place to Derek Warwick, but he preferred to stay with Renault.

Toleman was the real victim of the musical chairs, and their dilemma was to have long-term implications. Only when the management agreed to sign up with the Italian fashion house, Benetton, as sponsors, did Pirelli agree to re-supply tyres. Within a year, Benetton bought the whole team and the cars were renamed Benetton's, and soon after that they were challenging for a place at the top of Formula One.

For Senna, Lotus was the team to belong to. Unlike Toleman, it was rooted in the history of Formula One. Colin Chapman had gone, but Gerard Ducarouge had replaced him and there was a new car, the 97T. Lotus had produced a string of World Champions — Jim Clark, Graham Hill, Jochen Rindt, Mario Andretti, and above all, the man who paved the way for wave upon wave of boys from Brazil, Emerson Fittipaldi; the name meant something in Brazil. Getting Senna was also something of a coup for Lotus, the obvious up-and-coming driver. Elio de Angelis had been at Lotus for five seasons, and he had seen them through the years following Chapman's death. He was universally liked, both inside the team and beyond, and he had finished third in the 1984 World Championship, but he had still only won the single Grand Prix. There was no hostility when Senna joined de Angelis, but the new boy, with one year in Formula One, began to assert himself quietly inside the team, demanding here, cajoling there, steadily taking the attention of everybody he needed.

Once again the opening Grand Prix of the season was in Brazil, but once again he had bad luck in front of the family, retiring with an electrical problem; de Angelis came third.

The second event was at Estoril in Portugal. The Lotus 97T was on top form, being timed through the speed trap at the start/finish line at 192.434 mph, with only Nelson Piquet's Brabham-BMW faster. When it was reliable, Senna had found in the Lotus, a car which matched his skill and he managed to put it on pole position, the first time he had taken pole in Formula One, with 1 minute 21.007 seconds, some 2.5 seconds ahead of Piquet who was in seventh place. De Angelis, in the same car, was fourth on the grid

with 1 minute 22.159 seconds — any doubts about who was the No.1 driver at Lotus were fading.

Race day dawned with leaden skies and at the start it was raining heavily. Senna made a good start and went into the lead immediately. He was always happiest out in front, but in these conditions it was crucial, he was the only driver with a clear view ahead. Senna was in his element, and he began to pull away from Prost: 3 seconds by the end of the first lap, 12 seconds by the end of Lap 10. He was making the field, which included the three former World Champions — Lauda, Piquet and Rosberg — look a bit ordinary. He was also on Goodyear wet tyres, as were the McLaren, Ferrari, Renault and Williams drivers; Goodyear were much better than the Pirelli equivalents and the field was split along tyre lines — Piquet, who was on Pirellis, retired because his tyres were holding back so much. Senna was making even the other Goodyear-shod drivers look a bit slow: at the end of thirty laps, he was 30 seconds ahead.

The rain came down harder. Alain Prost, now 40 seconds behind Senna, aquaplaned on the finishing straight, spun, crashed into a wall and was out. Even Senna had had enough of the conditions, and each time he came round in front of the officials he waved his arms above his head, indicating that it should be stopped. With two of the sixty-nine laps to go, the officials gave in and stopped the race. Senna won by 1 minute 32 seconds from Michele Alboreto for Ferrari; they were the only drivers on the same lap at the end.

The Lotus pit crew leapt into the air, scrambled over the pit wall and surrounded the car in great excitement. It was the first time a Lotus had won a Grand Prix since Elio de Angelis' only victory at Imola in 1982. Things were looking up, they could feel they

Portugese Grand Prix, Estoril, 21 April 1985: dubbed the 'Regenmeister' for his prowess in the wet, Ayrton Senna led the whole race, bringing new hope to Lotus.

Career landmark:
Ayrton Senna's
first time on the
winners' podium
at Estoril
following his first
Grand Prix
victory in his
home from home,
Portugal.

had a winning driver in Ayrton Senna and those who could remember the days in 1978 when Mario Andretti won everything for Lotus, sensed that they could be on their way to a championship. It was also the first victory win since the death of Colin Chapman and for a moment it seemed that Senna had lifted the blight of his sudden departure.

It was Senna's seventeenth Grand Prix and he left his stamp all over it. He had started from pole position, had led from start to finish, taken fastest lap and won – no better way to mark his first victory in the World Championship. It put him equal second with Alain Prost, three points behind Alboreto. Senna's comment on the race was: 'I won today because my car gave me no trouble…and I made no mistakes.'

Two weeks later, he took pole position at the San Marino Grand Prix at Imola, and after a titanic struggle with Prost, dominated the race as he had done at Estoril until he ran out of fuel with four laps to go. Prost won, but was later disqualified, making Elio de Angelis the winner, only his second victory in seven years. Senna continued his hard driving, rarely off the front row of the grid, but he retired from the next five races and finished well down because of mechanical problems in others, so missing out on the points. At the end of the season, Prost won the Championship. Senna was fourth and de Angelis fifth.

The points did not tell the full story. His retirements had cost him dearly: when he had no mechanical problems and finished he was invariably in the first three. He won the Belgian Grand Prix, came second in the European Grand Prix at Brands Hatch, second in Austria, then third in the Dutch and Italian events; he had taken six pole positions and two fastest laps. De Angelis had finished more races, but he was often a lap behind the leaders. Quite simply, Senna put him in the shade, both on the track and in the team.

De Angelis was a popular, gregarious figure, but he was content simply to do his best – Senna was distant, a loner, but he was out to win. When the musical chairs started again, and after seven seasons at Lotus, de Angelis looked elsewhere. Honda, which was supplying engines to Williams helped get Piquet to move from Brabham to Williams, leaving a space at Brabham which de Angelis promptly filled. With his departure, however, there was a space at Lotus.

Renault had pulled out of racing its own team, though they continued to supply engines to Lotus, and the decision left Derek Warwick without a drive. He was quick, immensely popular in Britain, and Peter Warr wanted him to replace de Angelis, arranging a test drive at Brands Hatch. But this time, Senna had more power: Lotus needed him more than he needed Lotus, and he barred Warwick from the team. There was an outcry in the British press, the principal accusation being that Senna was scared of the competition. But Senna was not afraid of competition on the track, he thrived on it, what he was afraid of was Lotus spreading its resources too thinly while trying to support two drivers. He wanted the whole team focused on him. He knew the team from the inside, and he could see that Warwick would only diminish his own chances of winning the Championship. He wanted somebody who would not distract the team from that simple objective. Peter Warr was caught between a rock and a hard place. He wanted Senna more than he wanted Warwick, he knew that Senna could always find that extra little bit of speed when the car was at its limit, he had seen it. In a tough decision he turned Warwick down. One man's

Over: European Grand Prix, Brands Hatch, 6 October 1985; Senna under pressure from Keke Rosberg in the more powerful Williams-Honda; Senna held second place.

disappointment was another's opportunity: Senna then agreed to Johnny Dumfries, who was just graduating from Formula Three, as the second driver.

It was a ruthless decision on Senna's part, and a selfish decision, but if the single objective was winning, then it was a right decision and, like Toleman, Derek Warwick became one of the casualties of the inexorable rise of Ayrton Senna. When the music did stop, Warwick had no seat, and he briefly left Formula One to drive Jaguar sports cars. In an ironic and sad end to the musical chairs of the 1985 season, Warwick eventually joined Brabham four races into the 1986 season, replacing Elio de Angelis who had been killed in a crash testing a radical, new Brabham at Paul Ricard in France.

The mid 1980s saw the output from the turbocharged engine rising relentlessly, peaking with the BMW which touched 1300 bhp in qualifying form in 1986. The regulating bodies were concerned to limit such awesome power, and for 1986 they reduced the amount of fuel for a race from 220 to 195 litres. This forced the engine designers to choose between power and fuel consumption; drivers would no longer be able to flick the boost switch for an extra 100 bhp without taking the risk of running out of fuel. Honda, TAG-Porsche and Renault, who supplied the top teams of Williams, McLaren and Lotus respectively, responded with more fuel efficient engines, but Honda did the best job and the Williams FW11 was acknowledged as having the best balance between power and economy. Senna was now at a disadvantage: he would no longer be able to use the full potential of the engine without risking running out of fuel.

The rules did not apply in qualifying. At Rio, for the first race of the season, Senna put in his usual maximum effort in qualifying, taking pole position, and beating Nelson Piquet in front of their home crowd. In the race, though, he was handicapped and on Lap 1 Piquet went ahead, sandwiching Senna between the two Williams. Mansell tried to pass Senna at every opportunity, and in the process went into the barrier. Senna then tried everything he knew, within the fuel limits, to pass Piquet, but it was a question of mathematics and he simply could not do it. He had to settle for second place, his tanks dry. The one consolation was that he had put in a good performance for his ever loyal family.

The race proved what many had long suspected, that the FW11 was well ahead of the rest. If Senna was going to have any realistic chance of taking the Championship now, he would need a little luck and huge reserves of skill. His chance to show that he was the best, when no driver had a wide margin in performance, came in the Spanish Grand Prix on a new circuit at Jerez a couple of weeks later. It was a circuit which should favour the Lotus, with plenty of corners and not many straights where the Williams' power advantage could be used. The track designers' computer predictions suggested that the top speed would be 165 mph – Senna was timed through the speed trap at 182 mph. The same computer said that the fastest lap would be around 1 minute 52 seconds, Senna put in the fastest lap in both qualifying sessions, taking pole position with 1 minute 21.605 seconds. Even with the extra power of the Williams' car, Piquet could only manage 1 minute 22.431 seconds, with Mansell and Prost just behind that.

There were signs at Jerez that Senna was getting under the skin of the other drivers. The strong feelings over the way he had kept Derek Warwick out of the

Brazilian Grand Prix, Rio, 23 March 1986: a turbo fire as Senna puts the Lotus 98T under pressure in qualifying against the much improved Williams-Honda FW11.

team persisted, and there was still a rumbling controversy following the accident with Mansell in Rio. In *Autosport's* report on Spain, an unnamed driver was quoted as saying before the race: 'Senna seems to make up his own rules, so perhaps we will all have to play by them.'

Senna used pole position to make a good start, leading Piquet and Mansell into the first corner, followed by the two McLaren's of Alain Prost and Keke Rosberg. The five leading cars were driven by three former World Champions and the two strongest challengers. The winding circuit evened out the differences between the cars, and from the beginning, it was clearly going to be a close race, though Mansell dropped back a little because he was having problems with his fuel readout.

Elio de Angelis came into the Brabham pit on Lap 16, coming out again just ahead of the leading pack. If Senna slowed down, it might give the Williams' drivers just the opportunity they needed to pass him. So, characteristically he took the hard way out, going flat out as they approached the second corner and taking the inside line. De Angelis did not see him and pulled across, putting Senna on the grass. But still he would not slow down, keeping his foot down hard and showering his ex-team mate with stones as he went through. De Angelis then held up the others and Senna used the traffic to pull ahead by 2 seconds.

By Lap 30 he had stretched his lead to 3 seconds, but Mansell had sorted out his fuel calculations and was lying in third. On Lap 33 Mansell passed Piquet, nominally the Williams team's No.1 driver, and he began to claw back Senna's lead. On Lap 40 the gap between them was tiny when they came up to lap Martin Brundle on the pit straight. Senna was right

behind Brundle as they approached the right hander at the end of the straight, but Mansell was alongside too, taking the corner on the inside to go into the lead.

The gloves were off. First Senna tried to take Mansell on the outside, but Mansell held his line and Senna had to brake sharply, smoke pouring from his tyres. Then he tried again, this time on a hairpin where they had to slow right down. Senna managed to get on the inside, making Mansell lift off slightly, but in such close racing, the small loss of momentum was enough to let both Senna and Prost through. On the same lap, Piquet retired with a blown engine. With little to lose, Mansell came in for fresh tyres and rejoined the race 20 seconds behind in third place. All three drivers had fuel, but Mansell had the benefit of fresh rubber. With six laps to go, Mansell took Prost, who was defending second place. Then he caught up with Senna on the last lap. Both drivers used maximum boost, and as they approached the chequered flag Mansell pulled alongside Senna with his extra power. As they crossed the finish line, however, Senna just managed to hold Mansell off, by 0.014 of a second.

It was a classic motor race. The nature of the track diminished the value of the extra power of the Williams to the point where Senna's skill could overcome the difference. Senna was physically exhausted, but he was now leading the World Championship with 15 points to Piquet's 9 points.

Ayrton Senna was still a newcomer, but when he arrived for the round of motor racing ceremonies and parties, the room would hush slightly, eyes would turn, adding to the air of mystery about him. He attracted attention. He was of the Formula One family now, something of a black sheep still, but with four wins he was clearly established. He was intriguing to other drivers, and a threat; they were wary of him and that is just as he wanted it.

He drove hard, throughout the season, taking eight pole positions, and winning in Detroit, all the time in the knowledge that he was at a disadvantage. Nobody had seen at quite such close quarters just how much the season belonged to Williams and Honda, Mansell winning five races, to Piquet's four.

Prost took the Championship, much to the disappointment of Honda, who could not understand why Mansell had been allowed to challenge Piquet, their chosen candidate, from inside the same team, splitting the points. In 1987 there would be a Japanese Grand Prix for the first time since 1977, and Honda

was putting everything into Formula One, and they wanted their driver to win. The Williams' approach sowed the seeds of rumbling controversy which came to a head when the musical chairs started for 1987 and Honda offered Frank Williams a Japanese driver, Saturo Nakajima, to replace Mansell. They wanted to give Japanese drivers experience of Formula One and lessen the internal challenge to their chosen man, Piquet. Frank Williams stuck by Mansell, so Honda made Lotus an offer they could hardly refuse: Nakajima and the Honda engine. Peter Warr accepted and Johnny Dumfries' Formula One career was over.

The musical chairs ended with Piquet and Mansell staying at Williams, their relationship strained by

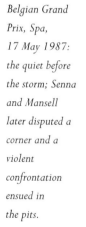

Belgian Grand Prix, Spa, 17 May 1987: the quiet before the storm; Senna and Mansell later disputed a corner and a violent confrontation ensued in the pits.

competing efforts to win the Championship. The problem of having two drivers competing in the same team was also evident at McLaren, where Prost and Rosberg, both former champions, could not coexist: Prost stayed and Rosberg retired. Senna signed on for a third season with Lotus, but he could see that the Renault engine was not as competitive as the Honda. He could also see the way Honda wanted to operate, and it mirrored his approach. They both wanted all the resources of a team concentrated on one driver, the only point of difference was that Senna was firmly convinced it should be him.

Senna still brought a sense of excitement to the Lotus team, a feeling that they could really achieve something, and there were great hopes for the new Lotus 99T which had been built in the company's tradition of innovation. It had computer-controlled active suspension, which ironed out the bumps in the circuit, but the aerodynamics were not as good as the Williams' FW11B which was less complicated and aerodynamically superb. Once again Williams had come up with the superior car, and the theme of the year was clearly going to be the battle between Mansell, in the slightly better car, and Senna, with his reserves of skill – a battle between two men who would try everything to win.

Senna put in a good performance in the Brazilian Grand Prix, but the family was once more denied a home victory when he retired with mechanical failure. At Imola, Mansell had the extra power to put him in second place. At Spa, for the Belgian Grand Prix, Mansell initially took the lead, but the race had to be restarted after an accident. Senna then took the lead with Mansell close behind and as they came to a right-hander, Mansell moved to the outside, on to the racing line, to overtake. Senna stayed where he was, and as they went into the corner neither would give way: they came together, their wheels touched and they both spun off. Senna was out, but Mansell rejoined and drove another seventeen laps before retiring.

When he got back to the pits, all the simmering resentment born of numerous super-competitive moments on the track bubbled over. Mansell went straight to the Lotus pit, where he found Senna and grabbed him fiercely. Mansell was furious and it showed – it took three Lotus mechanics to separate them. Whatever Senna felt, he kept it to himself, simply observing: 'When a man holds you round the throat, I do not think he has come to apologize.'

At Monaco they were alongside each other on the front row of the grid, Mansell on pole. He led for twenty-nine laps, then retired with mechanical problems. Senna inherited the lead and won, putting him just 3 points behind Alain Prost in the Championship; Piquet was third.

So it continued. Senna won the US Grand Prix when Mansell retired with cramp, having been in the lead. Senna had 27 points to Prost's 26 and Piquet's 24. Prost and Piquet had made up ground in the Championship with second and third places, when Mansell suddenly found form in the British Grand Prix and moved up to 1 point behind Senna. It was an exciting Championship, with any one of four star drivers in contention for the title, but it also seemed to Senna that he could only win when the Williams' drivers had problems, and that frustrated him.

At the German Grand Prix, Senna had made up his mind to leave Lotus. He had read between the lines, and he could see that of the three top teams, even with the Honda engine, Lotus was the third strongest, and

In three years, Senna won six Grands Prix for Lotus, came second in ten and third in six more, but mechanical failure in thirteen made him decide to move on.

Over: Monaco Grand Prix, 31 May 1987: Ayrton Senna on his way to his first victory on the classic street circuit; he was to win six times at Monte Carlo.

Brazilian Grand Prix, Rio, 3 April 1988: a reflective moment in the build up to Senna's first Grand Prix — on his home tarmac, in front of his family.

that only his driving performance was putting them in the serious points. So when the musical chairs started for the 1988 season, Senna got in early. At Hockenheim, he told Peter Warr that he would not be driving for Lotus the following year and began talks with McLaren in earnest.

Peter Warr was not idle. Between the German and Hungarian Grands Prix he signed up Nelson Piquet from Williams, effectively blocking any return had Senna wanted to change his mind.

Senna didn't mind, he was supremely confident in his ability, and convinced that he would get the drive he wanted for 1988. Behind the scenes the hand of Honda was at work. They could not support three top teams and having lost their patience with Williams, they decided to stop supplying them and joined forces with McLaren, while still supporting Lotus with Nakajima and Piquet.

The announcement that Ayrton Senna would join McLaren, and that he and Prost would have the Honda engine, was made at the Italian Grand Prix at Monza and it was smiles all round as the McLaren team boss Ron Dennis, Prost and Senna posed for photographers. Williams on the other hand, who had just delivered the World Champion and had lost both him and their winning engine in a series of ruthless decisions, were devastated. Honda had cast them aside, and though they received financial compensation, they would have to start from scratch again.

For Ayrton Senna it was the biggest step, and the biggest coup, of his career.

CHAPTER FIVE

WORLD CHAMPION

Every Formula One boss dreams of putting together a team with the perfect combination: the best cars, conceived by the best designers, using the most powerful engines, nurtured by the best mechanics and driven by the best drivers – all at the expense of a number of sponsors with long pockets. The art in the job is to juggle with a wide range of potentially conflicting and explosive ingredients without causing an explosion. Daily, the boss must reconcile the irreconcilable, the needs of safety with the need to win, the demands of engineers with the financial limits of the sponsors, and above all, the volatile emotions, limitless aspirations and huge egos of two world class drivers, possibly the most explosive mixture of all.

The quietly spoken, but iron-willed Ron Dennis is one such boss. Under his leadership, McLaren had grown in size and stature through the 1980s, taking the Constructors' title in 1984 and 1985, and giving Alain Prost two World Championships in 1985 and 1986. In 1987, McLaren's progress had faltered as Frank Williams took a commanding position in Formula One with his FW11B which brought together the superb Honda V-6 engine with two highly competitive drivers, Nelson Piquet and Nigel Mansell.

In seeking to make a giant leap forward in 1988, Dennis had secured the ingredients of that dream team: he had Gordon Murray, a gifted designer who had joined McLaren following the departure of original MP4 designer, John Barnard, to Ferrari; he had the Honda engine; he had Alain Prost; and to replace Stefan Johansson, whose 1987 season had been lacklustre, he had Ayrton Senna.

It was a breathtaking combination even for a boss of Dennis' calibre, bringing together as it did, under one roof, the two most competitive drivers in the Championship. Prost did not stand in the way of Senna joining the team, but he must have known that having two such dedicated winners in the same team was bound to produce some volatile situations. Neither driver was going to easily take second place to the other and both badly wanted to be World Champion, Prost for the third time, Senna for the first.

The courtship between Senna and Dennis had not been long – both men wanted the deal – but the negotiations had been arduous; Senna was as hard and uncompromising in business as he was on the track. When the discussions reached stalemate, with Senna and Dennis still far apart, it was Dennis who suggested they toss a coin for the difference and Senna agreed. Senna lost, and said later that it cost him £1 million over the three-year deal they then struck.

McLaren's Dream team: (left to right) Ron Dennis, visionary team manager, Alain Prost, double World Champion, and Ayrton Senna, the fastest newcomer for a generation.

Joining McLaren was a landmark in Ayrton Senna's career. He became part of the team just as it was blossoming into the supreme combination which Honda had judged could make the best use of their V-6. It was the last year of the turbocharged era and most engine manufacturers were looking to produce normally-aspirated engines for 1989. Honda put maximum effort into the RA-168E for 1988. Any doubts about the supremacy of the new McLaren-Honda MP4/4 were settled in the first testing session.

Prost went out first at Imola, putting in faster times than all the other teams. Then Senna tried it, easily mastering the new car and turning in laps around a second faster than Prost. The test had an electrifying effect on the whole team. Having drivers who deliver results makes a team even keener to deliver the car, and the joy of having not one but two drivers who could deliver the MP4/4's full potential, sent morale soaring. The idea that anything was possible pervaded McLaren as the team went home to England.

McLaren team spirit at the 1988 Spanish Grand Prix: they had already won the Constructors' title and either Prost or Senna would be World Champion.

If Ron Dennis could hold them together without exploding, he had come close to that perfect combination of ingredients and it made McLaren look and feel invincible.

The first Grand Prix of 1988 was once again in Rio. Senna had failed to win his country's Grand Prix in four years of trying and when he took pole position from Prost, the crowd was ecstatic. Euphoria turned to gloom as the green light came on and he remained stuck on the grid with gearbox problems. The race was restarted, with Senna driving a spare car from the pit lane, and he gave an astonishing display of the potential which Dennis had recognized, by moving from last place to second in twenty laps, behind Prost. The crowd savoured the possibility of a truly great race and the possibility of a home win.

It was not to be. During a pit stop he stalled and fell back to sixth place. Worse was to follow: unknown to Senna, Ron Dennis was arguing with officials about the start. Senna had changed cars after the green light, and the rules said that he could not start in a spare car in those circumstances, so he was disqualified. Prost won, but Senna's performance left little doubt where the fiercest competition would be coming from for the rest of the season.

At Imola, Prost was faster in the first qualifying session, but Senna took pole position in the second, then led the race from start to finish with Prost second. In the MP4/4, Senna had found the car to match his capability, they were perfectly in tune, and at Monaco two weeks later the bond became even stronger, far beyond his previous experience. He took pole position, and in later qualifying he went out to better his time. It was a special drive for him, something deep inside, an instinct, a level of driving skill he had never achieved before, took over. He described it later as a force beyond his conscious understanding: he was driving beyond the limit, detached from the reality around him, the road ahead part of a continuous tunnel. His lap speeds went up and up, until he was 2 seconds ahead of Prost, before he returned to reality and slowed down.

The metaphysical experience returned for the race. The two McLarens were well ahead of the rest of the field, with Senna leading Prost by a staggering 50 seconds on Lap 66. There was no reason to be going so fast and team orders were sent out to ease off. Lap times dropped off by 3 seconds for both of them, but the effect on Senna was negative; he lost the strange sense of detachment and with it his concentration; he misjudged a corner, clipping the Armco at the apex with the right-hand nose fin, spinning the car round and into the barrier on the opposite side of the track. He was unhurt but shaken and he did not want to talk to anybody. Instead of making his way back to the pits, he stepped over the barrier and went home to his Monte Carlo flat.

The crash was put down to 'brain fade', an expression used to describe the loss of the intense concentration which all drivers depend on when driving at the limit. Senna believed he was beyond the limit, drawing on previously untapped levels of concentration, and from that experience he traced a change not only in his career, but in the direction of his life. He had been brought up as a Christian, but had moved from his Christianity in the course of his young adult life. The experience at Monaco was very special to him and it brought back a devotion to his faith, and he made no secret of his belief in God as a guiding force in his life.

Monaco Grand Prix, 15 May 1988: Ayrton Senna in the lead and driving beyond the limit before he lost his concentration and crashed into a barrier.

After the race, Senna was visited by his sister, Viviane, and his mother. Viviane was a psychologist by profession, but she was also an evangelical Christian. Her father-in-law was a leading evangelical priest in Sao Paulo, and she was very open about her Christianity. Both women had a strong influence over Ayrton Senna and they urged him to find guidance and strength in the New Testament; the word of God began to play an increasingly important part in his life.

Prost won at Monaco, giving McLaren the first three races of the season, two to Prost and one to Senna. Senna had retired from two races, so Prost was ahead in the Championship table: Prost 24, Gerhard Berger 14 and Senna 9. Over the next eight races, the mood changed as Senna put his stamp on the whole Formula One circus as nobody had done since the days of Jim Clark and before that Stirling Moss and Juan Manuel Fangio. Though he was actually leading the Championship, Prost began to look like the supporting cast. He won in Mexico with Senna second, putting Prost on 33 points to Berger's 18 and Senna's 15. Then Senna won in Canada, with Prost second. In the United States Grand Prix in Detroit, Senna took his sixth straight pole position, equalling the record of Stirling Moss in 1959/60 and Lauda in 1974. Berger was forced to retire in both races so Senna moved up to 13 points behind Prost.

Prost then won in France with Senna second, then Senna won the British Grand Prix, his fourth victory of the season. Prost had retired in the wet weather and he came in for loud criticism from the French press which suggested that he was no longer hungry enough. He answered them by winning in Germany with Senna second. They were out on their own in the Championship, but the gap between them was only

3 points: Prost 60, Senna 57. They were so far ahead of the competition that Honda could relax: one of their drivers was going to be World Champion.

They had a terrific battle in Hungary, nearly fulfilling the team manager's worst nightmare when they refused to give way at one corner and nearly touched. Senna won by 0.5 seconds, his sixth victory in a season and equalling Jim Clark's record which had stood for twenty years. It also put him on a par with Prost with 66 points each, and when Senna won at Spa, he led the Championship table for the first time that year by 75 points to 72 and gave McLaren the Constructor's title.

The pressure on both men was intense. Senna took yet another pole position in the Italian Grand Prix, his tenth for the season and another record. He led the race but, having barely skipped a beat all season, Prost's engine failed and he retired. On their home ground, the two Ferraris of Gerhard Berger and Michele Alboreto were putting Senna under pressure. With only a few laps to go he was about to lap Jean-Louis Schlesser as they came up to the chicane when Schlesser lost control. Instead of waiting, Senna went for the gap just as Schlesser's Williams bounced back into his path. The pressure was showing. He could have waited but with the Ferrari in his wing mirrors he had taken a chance and collided with Schlesser. For the first time that year, there was no McLaren driver on the podium.

At Estoril, Senna took the lead from the start with Prost just behind. As they completed the first lap, coming into the pit straight, Prost moved alongside him to overtake. They were doing around 190 mph, but rather than let him past, Senna moved towards the other McLaren. Prost moved closer to the pit wall, but

British Grand Prix, Silverstone, 10 July 1988: Senna won; his control in the rain helped him eclipse his team mate Alain Prost who disliked the wet.

Senna kept coming. Prost said later that he could not lift off, because the cars were so close he risked hitting Senna's rear wheel. Senna had deliberately created a potentially lethal situation for both of them rather than give way. The danger was palpable, and as the cars sped past the wall, the mechanics and pit onlookers leapt back, fearing the worst.

The pressure was getting to both of them. Later in the race, Senna had to back off to conserve fuel, and Prost won; Senna finished sixth. Prost had seen a dark side of Senna, the darkest possible side, somebody who had made it plain by his actions that there were no limits to what he would do to win. It was a chilling reminder, if one was needed, of how hard he could be, and when being hard was not enough, how dirty he could be. It was a dangerous business, but Prost had more respect for life: 'OK,' he said after the race, 'if he wants the Championship that badly, he can have it.'

The relationship between the two McLaren drivers remained professional, cordial even, at least on the surface, but the McLaren MP4 was so much quicker than the competition that they only had each other to race. This produced incidents, such as Estoril, and underneath the relationship was becoming severely frayed at the edges.

Senna took pole position in Spain, but Prost won. Senna was fourth, putting him 5 points behind in the title race. But the points system worked in Senna's favour – only the best eleven results counted, so with fourteen races run, each driver had to discard three. Prost had finished more races in the points and was punished for his consistency, while Senna could discard races where he had not finished. With two races to go, the Japanese and the Australian Grands Prix, Senna could become World Champion by winning only the Japanese Grand Prix, even though Prost had accumulated more points in the season.

Such a finely balanced, and seemingly unfair, position brought out all the edginess and latent paranoia in the Championship. Inevitably, with the attention focused on just two drivers in identical cars, the sport began to split along nationalistic, commercial and emotional lines. Prost had won two Championships already, so there was a faction who supported Senna the underdog. Others, remembering the way Senna had found his way to the top, supported Prost. In France and Brazil the support was rather more predictable. Any excuses for paranoid feelings were leapt on, and one conspiracy theory which gained great currency was that Honda favoured Senna, and that he was receiving favourable treatment in the engine department. It reached the point that Jean-Marie Balestre the President of FIA, the Federation Internationale de L'Automobile, was moved to take it up directly with Honda in an exchange of letters with its President, Tadashi Kume. Balestre sought assurances that the two drivers were receiving equal treatment, and he got it, but the exchange did little to damp down the already volatile situation inside McLaren as they prepared for the Japanese Grand Prix.

Senna dominated qualifying at Suzuka, taking his twelfth pole position of the season. Then at the start of the race he had a disaster: he stalled. Fortunately for him the start was on a slight incline and he had generated just enough momentum to bump start the McLaren, setting off at the back of the grid. The first lap was pure aggression. He finished it 13 seconds behind Prost in eighth place.

It took ten laps and a series of sublime manoeuvres by Senna, to pass RiccardoPatrese's Williams, the two

Benettons of Alessandro Nannini and Thierry Boutsen, and the two Ferraris of Michele Alboreto and Gerhard Berger, to lie third, only Ivan Capelli in a March between him and Prost. It began to drizzle, dampening the track.

On Lap 20, Capelli's engine misfired and he was forced to retire. Senna and Prost were out on their own in a very personal battle for the Championship. The drizzle stopped. Prost held on, but as they approached the chicane, just before the finishing straight on Lap 27, they came up to lap Mauricio Gugelmin and Andrea de Cesaris who were fighting for twelfth place. Prost was unlucky and had to slow as they went into the chicane. Arriving just that little bit later, Senna could keep his momentum up, and coming out of the chicane he used this slight advantage together with maximum power down the straight to take the best line on turn one and quickly pulled ahead of Prost by 2.5 seconds.

Then it began to rain. Prost kept up the challenge, clawing back a second here, losing it there, then coming back. With some irony, Senna pointed to the sky each time he passed the line, reminding officials, and anybody else, that in Monaco in 1984 when the situation was the other way round, they had stopped the race. He won it the hard way, juggling his fuel consumption, his lead and the weather perfectly. Coming out of the chicane on the last lap, the chequered flag only seconds away, the stress began to lift and an inner sense of elation went through him. In his own account of those last few seconds of the race he said that he looked up and among the rain clouds he had a clear vision of God.

Ayrton Senna, the boy from Brazil, was World Champion, and he had done it in some style: he had taken pole, driven the fastest lap, won the race by 13

seconds, his eighth win in the season breaking the record set by Jim Clark in 1963 and equalled by Alain Prost in 1984; there were tears in his eyes as he accepted his congratulations.

In Brazil there was wild celebration as he gave his post-race interview on television, and he returned to Sao Paulo a national hero on the scale of Pele and Emerson Fittipaldi.

The mid-1980s were a period of change in Brazil: the military government had been replaced by a democratically elected president, and in its effort to rid itself of chronic inflation, Brazil had a new pride in itself, a pride into which Ayrton Senna, the new World Champion, fitted perfectly. By comparison with other great Brazilian sportsmen he was intensely patriotic. Many of them, once they had established themselves on the international scene, moved abroad. Even Pele had moved to New York to join Cosmos, and the steady stream of Brazilian footballers who went to play for Italian clubs lived in Italy. Joachim Cruz, Brazil's 800 metre gold medallist in the 1984 Olympic Games in Los Angeles had gone to live in the US where he could earn more money and enhance his career, and Nelson Piquet not only lived abroad, he even spoke Portuguese with an English accent.

Ayrton Senna was a hard currency multi-millionaire, earning around £15 million a year from racing alone. He could have lived anywhere in the world, but he chose to make his home in Brazil and returned to his family whenever he could. He had bought property and he had established his business headquarters in Sao Paulo and it was no public relations stunt. He wanted to be there when he could have been somewhere else. He was Brazilian to the core and Brazilians, rich and poor, loved him for that.

Japanese Grand Prix, Suzuka, 30 October 1988: pole position, fastest lap, race winner, World Champion for the first time, and a place in the history books.

Senna had always been a Christian, but as his success had grown, so he had found a need for a greater spiritual dimension to his life. He was not a churchgoer, he claimed to prefer to pray alone and on the long flights back and forward to Brazil, he read the New Testament and frequently alighted from the aircraft with the Bible in his hand.

He kept his private life very private, but at the end of his Championship year, the archetypal Brazilian hero fell in love with one of the most prominent women in Brazil, Xuxa Menguel, a television presenter. There had been a string of beautiful girlfriends since the end of his marriage, but they had never interfered with his life as a racing driver and his progress towards the World Championship, to which he had been utterly dedicated. His relationship with Xuxa seemed different; she was a prominent Brazilian, she had the

approval of his family, and it was the fervent hope of young Brazilians that they would marry.

Winning the 1989 Brazilian Grand Prix for the first time would have been a fairy tale beginning to the new season, and Senna raised hopes by taking pole position, proudly displaying the coveted number 1 on the front of his car before his family, friends and the home crowd. He made a good start, but so did Riccardo Patrese for Williams and Gerhard Berger for Ferrari, and the three were almost abreast going in to the first corner, with Senna sandwiched in the middle. He moved right, and Berger moved too, Patrese taking the inside line. Then Berger and Senna touched, leaving Senna's nose section badly damaged. He went into the pits losing a whole lap as it was replaced. He could not make up the time, and in front of a disappointed home audience, Nigel Mansell won with Prost second.

Mexican Grand Prix, 28 May 1989: Ayrton Senna winning from his thirty-third pole position, breaking the record set by Jim Clark twenty years previously.

To avoid the same thing happening between team mates, Prost and Senna had a general agreement that whichever of them made it to the first corner in the lead, would not be impeded by the other, enabling him to get away from the pack as quickly as possible. Senna was on pole at the San Marino Grand Prix, with Prost alongside him, and he made a clean start, going straight into the lead before the first corner. Then Gerhard Berger's Ferrari went off at Tamburello corner, catching fire. Miraculously, Berger escaped but the race had to be restarted.

This time Prost made the better start, and going into the first corner he believed he was not going to be challenged by Senna who was just behind. Senna interpreted their agreement differently. Before they started braking he felt it was legitimate to go for the racing line, which he did, taking the corner and going into the lead. Senna led for the rest of the race to win from Prost, the only two cars to complete the full fifty-eight laps. Prost was furious. He was so angry that he did not attend the post-race press conference, for which he was fined $5000, and he complained bitterly to Ron Dennis that their agreement had been broken. It looked as if he had been duped, and he was so upset that he even suggested to Dennis that he could no longer stay in the same team as Senna and would drop out of racing. Dennis had a strong relationship with Prost, going back six years, and he was developing a strong relationship with Senna. He talked at length to Senna to try and iron out the matter, but Senna maintained that because he had made his move before the braking area for the corner, that he was within the letter of the agreement with Prost, but under pressure from Dennis and 'for the good of the team', he apologized to Prost.

Dennis hoped the matter would rest there, but Prost was wounded and he found Senna was impossible to deal with. Senna's whole approach was adversarial; conflict was part of his approach to life, as well as his approach to racing, and Prost had really had enough. Before the next Grand Prix, Prost gave an interview to the French motor magazine *L'Equipe* making it public and plain that in his view the relationship between him and Senna had broken down: 'at the level of technical discussion I shall not close the door completely, but for the rest I no longer wish to have any business with him. I appreciate honesty and he is not honest.'

The interview was the hot topic at Monaco, but Senna did not react, he kept is own council. His comment came with his driving: he took pole, won the race followed by victory in Mexico, too.

Then Senna's performance went into a decline. He retired from the United States Grand Prix, which Prost won and drove a magnificent race in Canada, only for the engine to fail. Prost was winning again, but the feeling that he was not getting equal treatment with Senna inside the team was growing, and eating away at him. He won the French Grand Prix, and Senna retired putting him 20 points ahead in the World Championship, but he had decided that he would leave McLaren at the end of the season.

At Silverstone for the British Grand Prix, Senna took pole position and made a good start, powering past Prost with little space between them, and into the lead. Then his gearbox failed and he spun off. Senna's reputation as a driver was formidable, but as a sportsman and as an individual it was at an all-time low and when the news of his misfortune reached the grandstands, the British crowd cheered. Senna fought back the only way he ever did, with wins in both the Germany and Belgium Grands Prix, reducing his margin behind Prost to 11 points.

Prost won the Italian Grand Prix, then announced that he was leaving McLaren to join Ferrari. The atmosphere in the World Championship was sour. Prost could not wait to leave the team he had served for six years, for whom he had won two Drivers' Championships and was now on the verge of winning a third. Senna took pole position at Estoril and went into the lead. On Lap 39 Mansell came down the pit lane but missed his pit, needing to put his car in reverse to get there, against the rules. He should have known that he would be disqualified, but he rejoined behind Senna. The black flag came out, telling Mansell to come in, but he failed to see it so intent was he on catching Senna. Coming up the finishing straight Mansell went to overtake and positioned himself on the inside for the first corner. Senna was just in front when he turned in and neither gave way. They collided, and Senna spun off into a sand trap. Berger won and Prost was second, putting him 24 points ahead in the Championship. Mansell was fined $50,000 and suspended for the next race.

British Grand Prix, 16 July 1989: in an informal moment, the World Champion takes time to greet his Brazilian fans in the grandstands at Silverstone.

After the race, Prost made no secret of his feelings that Senna had been getting preferential treatment from McLaren, especially in regard to the engines. His comments prompted McLaren to issue a statement with his name attached to it to the effect that there was no problem. However, it made little difference to the public's perception that Prost was leaving McLaren because Ayrton Senna was the favoured driver, effectively No.1 in the team.

Senna suffered a personal loss in the year, his publicist, business colleague and friend, Armando Boteilho, died of liver cancer which seemed to draw him even closer to his faith and his need for God. He chose Portugal to make a statement about his religious beliefs: 'I no longer feel awkward about talking about Him and if I am lucky enough to feel like this, my duty is to pass God's message on to others.... I have decided to spread the word in an open manner to those who are receptive to his teachings.'

Senna won in Spain, keeping alive his hopes of the Championship. Prost could win the title in Japan, but if Senna could win in both Japan and Adelaide, he could retain the title. Senna took pole position at Suzuka, his forty-first, but in the warm up Prost was quicker, giving the race a real air of edge and excitement: once again it looked likely that the year-long Championship battle between the two would be settled in Japan. Prost made the better start, leading by 1.7 seconds at the end of the first lap, and by Lap 5 he had stretched it to 3.8 seconds. They both made pit stops, then Senna began to reel him in, until he had to lap Nelson Piquet who made sure that he was held up for a frustrating complete lap.

Once he was past, Senna broke the lap record catching up with Prost. With four laps to go, Senna had reduced the gap to 0.5 seconds and he worked out that the only place he was likely to get past Prost was at the chicane. As they approached it, Senna put two wheels on the grass and went for the inside line. As Prost turned in, Senna held his position and Prost, though he had given way before in such circumstances, did not do so this time. The inevitable happened: the cars collided and slid off the circuit together.

Prost got out in disgust, but Senna was gripped by a fierce will to win and he urged the track marshals to push start him. Then he used the escape road to get back into the race, stopped in the pits for a new nose cone and set off after Alessandro Nannini who had

taken the lead. He overtook Nannini as they passed Prost's stationary car and Senna crossed the line first.

Senna sat in his cockpit with tears welling in his eyes, he had given everything and in his view he had won. It was Nannini, however, who was announced as the winner, which meant that Senna had been disqualified and Prost was World Champion. Senna was fuming inside as they went to the post-race press conference where Prost went to shake his hand. Senna brushed the gesture aside.

Senna saw the decision as political; FISA and the motor racing establishment trying to frustrate his progress. Other drivers had missed corners or parts of them in other races and had not been disqualified. FISA also invoked other accidents in which Senna had been involved in support of the decision. Senna felt a deep sense of injustice and vowed to fight the decision. In Adelaide, where Prost withdrew because of rain and Senna crashed into the back of Martin Brundle and retired, he also made his feelings about the Formula One politics public: 'What we see today is true manipulation of the World Championship.'

In the view of FISA he had maligned the sport. The governing body fined him $100,000 and revoked his racing licence, suspending him for six months; McLaren lodged an appeal.

Portuguese Grand Prix, Estoril, 24 September 1989: following his collision with Nigel Mansell, Senna's hopes of a second consecutive World Championship slipped.

Alain Prost, and his relationship with McLaren for whom he had driven ninety-two Grands Prix, winning thirty of them, and the only driver who could be bracketed with Senna in terms of skill, had become casualties of the total commitment which Senna had to winning. They were completely different characters. Prost observed several times that Senna thrived on conflict and without the extraordinary, and determined, diplomatic qualities of Ron Dennis, Prost would probably have left the team earlier. He had been happy at McLaren for five years, and he had not stood in the way of Senna joining the team, but the way Senna then managed to focus the energies of the team on him off the track, and his relentless intimidation of him on the track, wore Prost down. Prost's ironic comment at the end of what had been a bitter season for him: 'Ayrton has one problem: he thinks he can't kill himself because he believes in God, and I think that's very dangerous for the other drivers.'

Senna did not see it that way at all and his winter in Brazil, normally a time of renewal, was one of discontent. He was a proud man, he believed he was in the right, and he refused to pay the fine imposed by FISA, or make the apology demanded by Jean-Marie Balestre, its president.

The sour atmosphere carried over into the preparations for the following season. Senna appeared in front of the World Motorsport Council on 7 December 1989. He accepted that he had made the comments, but declined to apologize or pay the fine. For a month nothing happened, so in January the Council released a press notice making public the fact that they had not received any communication from Senna, and saying that unless he complied with their decision, his Super Licence, needed to compete in

Grands Prix, would not be issued for the coming season. The deadline for nominations was 15 February and still nothing had been received. FISA then published the list of drivers for 1989 omitting Senna's name. An hour later, they issued another list with his name included, accompanied by part of a letter from Senna which Balestre accepted as an apology. This ended months of what most people in the sport saw as a very unseemly public row which did nothing to enhance the image of the World Championship.

FISA's list of drivers also revealed that Gerhard Berger had swapped places with Alain Prost, and would be Senna's new team mate at McLaren.

Senna took pole position at the US Grand Prix at Phoenix and won. Then he went back to Sao Paulo for his thirtieth birthday and, four days later, the Brazilian Grand Prix which had been moved from Rio to Interlagos. Jean-Marie Balestre, by now a hate figure in Brazil, arrived surrounded by bodyguards and when, as President of FISA, he made a speech, and chose to do so in Spanish, feelings against him ran even higher and he was drowned out by catcalls in Portugese. The Sao Paulo crowd's hostility to Balestre took many forms, but the most eloquent, which showed how low the level of argument had sunk, came from the street vendors who did a roaring trade in T-shirts with a picture of Senna's McLaren and underneath it, the slogan: 'F—- you Balestre'.

Senna had never won his home Grand Prix. He took pole position and made a good start, with his new team mate Berger in second place. As ever, his most eloquent moment came on the track, and as he opened up the gap between them on the first lap, the whole grandstand erupted; 70,000 voices raised in support of the local hero.

Family Man: in troubled times, Ayrton Senna invariably turned to his family for support. From right to left, his mother Neide, his younger brother Leonardo, Ayrton, his father Milton, his sister Vivianne and her husband and children.

Behind the two McLarens was Thierry Boutsen for Williams, then Senna's two implacable opponents, both in Ferrari red, Alain Prost and Nigel Mansell. Boutsen managed to get past Berger to challenge Senna, who responded by extending his lead, once again to enthusiastic cheers. Prost meantime was also going for Berger and passed him on Lap 17. Three laps later, Senna had to deal with the first of the back-markers. He stopped for tyres, but managed to get back in the race 12.5 seconds ahead of Prost, who was now lying second. Prost could not close the gap, but when Senna came up behind Saturo Nakajima's Tyrell, they collided when Nakajima, who was having handling problems, drifted in front of Senna's car, damaging the McLaren's nose cone. Senna went into the pits again, rejoining in third place. The new nose cone was not as well set up as the previous one, however, and he could not improve on his position, coming third behind Prost and Berger. Prost was smiling mightily on the winners' rostrum, his first victory for Ferrari, his fortieth Grand Prix victory, and all at the expense of Senna on his home tarmac.

The battle for the title between Prost and Senna continued in their different teams. Senna won at Monaco and in Canada, then Prost won in Mexico, France and Britain, putting him ahead. Senna fought back with wins in Germany, Belgium and Italy, putting him back in front again. Prost was second at Monza, but it began to look increasingly like a second Senna Championship. They had barely exchanged a word for a year, then in the press conference after the race, a journalist asked the simple and obvious question of whether they would ever be able to reconcile their personal differences. It put them both on the spot, and both made hesitant statements designed not to upset

the other. Then Prost extended his hand to Senna and Senna shook it warmly; they left clapping each other on the shoulders, to the applause of the press corps.

Nigel Mansell won in Portugal, with Senna second and Prost third, so to keep alive any hope of winning the Championship Prost had to win the next Grand Prix in Spain. It was a race marred in qualifying when the Lotus driver, Martin Donnelly, had a high-speed accident. Donnelly was thrown out of the car by the impact and lay motionless on the track. When the doctor and ambulance arrived, the expectation was that he was dead. Senna went over and stood close to where he lay, alone and pensive. Once Donnelly had been taken to hospital, Senna went back to the motor home, again alone, to sit and think. Either he had to drive, reasserting his confidence, or he had to drop out. He drove, and put in the fastest qualifying lap, a full second ahead of anybody else.

Donnelly survived his injuries and Senna went to visit him in hospital. Consciously or subconsciously, and despite the distance he always maintained between him and the other drivers, he was assuming the mantle of their unofficial leader, the first among equals, 'the man to beat'.

Prost won in Spain, putting the denouement of the Championship back to the Japanese Grand Prix again. It was the opposite of the situation in 1989, when Senna had everything to do; this time, Prost had to win. If Senna won, then he would be World Champion. If Prost won, then he could still technically take the title in the Australian Grand Prix. But there was a third scenario: if neither took any points away from Suzuka, then Senna was Champion.

Senna took pole position, then an argument broke out with FISA about which side of the track pole

Spanish Grand Prix, Jerez, 30 September 1990: a fan embroidered a cushion to commemorate Ayrton Senna's record fiftieth pole position.

Japanese Grand Prix, Suzuka, 21 October 1990: the start. Alain Prost (front right) just ahead of Ayrton Senna (front left) heading for the first corner.

position should be and the final decision went against Senna. He had to start from a spot on the racing line, which was covered in rubber from qualifying, while Prost, though slightly behind on the staggered grid, was on a clean piece of track which would give him more grip. Both made good starts, Prost just ahead, but Senna took the inside line and stayed there. They came into the first corner on a collision course and the inevitable happened; the two cars came together and slid off into a sand trap. The race was over for them, but Ayrton Senna was World Champion again.

The fragile peace between the two best drivers in Formula One was broken, and Prost attacked Senna: 'What he did was more than unsporting, it was disgusting…can you imagine what young drivers think when they see things like that…..they will think they can get away with anything.'

Ferrari was also furious and pointed out to FISA that it did not spend its money to go racing, only to have its cars shunted off the track. FISA announced that it would hold a special commission.

Ayrton Senna started the 1991 season with a win at Phoenix, then straight back home to Sao Paulo for the Brazilian Grand Prix at Interlagos, his ninth attempt to win the race. He took pole position and made a good start, but Nigel Mansell, now back at Williams, was driving an aggressive race and stayed second. After the pit stops, Senna had a lead of 7 seconds and Mansell then had to make a second pit stop to have a ripped tyre replaced. Then it began to rain. Mansell spun, removing the most obvious threat, but RiccardoPatrese took up the challenge. Then Senna's gearbox started to misbehave: he lost third, then fifth and finally, with Patrese closing, all he could find was sixth gear. He just held on to win. That night, several thousand

people surrounded his house in Sao Paulo and he had to have a police escort home. They would not leave until he appeared with the trophy.

With victories at Imola and Monaco, he won the first four races of the season, but there had been something of a renaissance at Williams who had built a superb car around the Renault engine and Mansell was the new challenger for the title in a car that was showing every indication of being more than a match for the McLaren MP4s. The advantage was soon visibly

Seconds after the start at Suzuka, Senna and Prost collide, ending the race for both of them and giving Ayrton Senna his second World Championship.

slipping away: in Canada Senna had an electrical fault and retired and Piquet won for his new team, Benetton. In Mexico, Senna could only manage third behind the two Williams' of Mansell and Patrese, and in France he was third again, behind Prost and Mansell. Mansell won the British Grand Prix, with Senna fourth, then in Germany, Senna and Prost were involved in an incident at the chicane which had left Prost nowhere to go except down an escape road and out of the race. Senna ran out of fuel and finished

seventh, out of the points, while Mansell won, putting him 8 points behind Senna in the Championship.

Senna then went through a renaissance: he took pole and won a brilliant victory in Hungary, followed by a repeat at Spa, Belgium, then came second to Mansell at Monza. The competition between Senna and Mansell was no less fierce than that with Prost, but it did not have the same bitter personal edge as with Prost. Mansell was still a challenger for the title, and he was leading at Estoril when he came in for tyres.

His hopes all but disappeared when the right rear wheel was not properly replaced and came off as he left the pits. Patrese won and Senna was second. Then Mansell won in Spain, with Senna fifth, narrowing the margin to Senna 85, Mansell 69.

The Championship was decided at Suzuka again when Mansell spun off, and Senna, the Championship his for the third time, showed rare magnanimity on the track. His engine was running a little rough, but he slowed right down, giving the race to his team mate Gerhard Berger.

Ten days before the race, Jean-Marie Balestre had been replaced as President of FISA by Max Mosley, a British lawyer and a co-founder of March. Senna used the opportunity of his third world title to pour out his feelings about the treatment he had received at the hands of FISA. He could not forget the perceived

injustices and they rankled deeply: 'I won this race in 1989 and was prevented from going on to the podium by Jean-Marie Balestre. I was robbed badly by the system and that I will never forget; 1989 was unforgivable and I still struggle to cope with that. They decided against me and that was not justice, so what took place over the winter was shit.'

The attack went on for some time and as it progressed, it became more liberally sprinkled with expletives. It covered the decision over pole position in the 1990 Japanese Grand Prix, and the point moments afterwards when many believed he had deliberately pushed Prost off at the first corner as an act of revenge for losing the Championship the previous year. In his attack, Senna came close to admitting it: 'I said to myself... if tomorrow Prost beats me off the line, at the first corner I will go for it, and he better not turn in because he is not going to make it.'

The departure of Balestre marked the end of an era and for Senna his outburst was a catharsis, the ridding of years of hate built up against the establishment. But he soon realized he had gone too far and after discussions with the new President, Max Mosley, he issued a statement which said that his remarks had been 'misinterpreted' and that at no time did he deliberately collide with Prost. Most commentators preferred to believe the original version.

The times were changing. Recession was shortening the pockets of sponsors, and the dream team which Ron Dennis had put together in 1988 was no longer as dominant. Senna had given them three world titles, but the cost had been high, both for Prost, and for the public image of Formula One which at times seemed more like a club for rich young men to trade insults rather than race cars against each other.

The fruits of success: Ayrton Senna taking time off from his gruelling World Championship schedule and the pressure of his growing business empire in Brazil.

World Champion 1991: Ayrton Senna with the most powerful men in Formula One, Max Mosley (extreme left), Jean-Marie Balestre and Bernard Ecclestone (extreme right).

CHAPTER SIX

A PLACE IN HISTORY

There has only ever been room for a tiny number of drivers at the top of Grand Prix racing. At any one time, the men who are genuinely competing for the top honours belong to an exclusive club of three, maybe four at the most. To thrive, they must be with the team with the best cars, and they are always on the lookout for any sign that another team has found a new designer, a new engine with a few more horsepower, or a gearbox which can take a fraction of a second off each gear change, anything which will give the opposition an edge.

Once there, they are anxious to stay with the top teams, who are equally keen to keep them for as long as their skills and their nerve do not desert them. But there are always new drivers who want to join that club, usually young men ready to elbow the existing members aside at the first opportunity.

Deciding who drives for which team is a political process of Byzantine proportions, involving secrecy, money, status, personal relationships and national considerations. Sometimes it works and the result is a dream combination like Ayrton Senna, Ron Dennis, McLaren and Honda, but it is not always so, and often the best driver does not get the best seat.

The three best drivers in 1991 were Ayrton Senna, Alain Prost and Nigel Mansell. As they raced each other for the Championship in 1991, they were also jostling for position in the 1992 season, and they did so against the background of changes in the relative fortunes of McLaren and Williams which had been dramatic. When Honda had switched from McLaren to Williams in 1988, Frank Williams had to look elsewhere for an engine. Initially he turned to Judd, but the team had a very bad season and Nigel Mansell left for Ferrari. In 1989, Williams changed to Renault,

and over three years the French car giant poured in enough money and expertise to develop a V-10 engine to challenge the dominance of Honda. It was the basis of the Williams FW14, which by 1991 had proved more than a match for the once all-conquering McLaren MP4 series. For 1992 it had evolved into the FW14B, and all three of the top drivers realized it was going to be hard to beat.

They eyed it with different emotions. Nigel Mansell, who had rejoined Williams for the 1991 season and driven the FW14 to second place in the Championship, was in possession and with the team working around him well was in no mood to share his car with any serious challenger for the title. Alain Prost, who had fallen out with Ferrari in the closing stages of 1991 over his outspokenness and had been sacked, saw only opportunity, thwarted by Mansell's tenure at Williams. Ayrton Senna, who had seen the best years of McLaren and had signed up for the 1992 season with them, saw the FW14B as a threat, and he was envious.

The dictum that getting into the right team is the first step towards winning the Championship was never more sharply focused. All three men would have liked to have been with Williams, but all three knew that no two of them could ever be in the same team and RiccardoPatrese stayed on as No. 2 at Williams.

Prost was offered a drive with the French team Ligier, but rather than accept a move to the second rank, he bowed out, taking a sabbatical year. The losers were the fans who would be denied the thrill of a three-cornered fight for the Championship by the three best drivers. His departure left a space in the exclusive club which was provisionally filled by Michael Schumacher driving for Benetton. Ford had

Monaco Grand Prix, 23 May 1993: Ayrton Senna at his formidable best on the streets of Monte Carlo to give him his sixth, record win in Formula One's premier race.

re-entered Formula One, supplying engines to the Benetton team, which was under the dynamic management of Flavio Briatore.

The MP4/7, McLaren's answer to the resurgence at Williams and the challenge from Benetton was not ready for the beginning of the 1992 season, so for the first races Senna and Gerhard Berger, with whom Senna managed to maintain a friendly relationship, had to use the previous year's car, the MP4/6. It soon became plain that Williams was in control and that the FW14B was going to make 1992 Mansell's year. The slaughter started in South Africa with first place going to Mansell, then Patrese, Senna, Schumacher. It continued in Mexico with Mansell first, then Patrese and Schumacher; Senna retired with transmission problems. In Brazil, on Senna's home track at Interlagos, it was the same story: Mansell, Patrese, Schumacher; the local hero forced to retire. At Imola, it was Mansell, Patrese, Senna.

The Monaco Grand Prix looked like going the same way as they lined up for the start: Mansell in pole position, Patrese second and Senna third. Then some of the magic flared in Senna and he managed to get between Mansell and Patrese at the start. Mansell began to pull away, and Senna was soon under pressure from Patrese. While he was holding off the second Williams, Mansell drew steadily away, establishing a lead of some 20 seconds. On Lap 60 Michele Alboreto spun and Senna came across his Footwork car sitting in the middle of the track and had to stop, costing him another ten seconds. Mansell looked unassailable until he had to come in for tyres at which time Senna just managed to get ahead before Mansell rejoined, the first time a car other than a Williams-Renault had led a Grand Prix that year.

French Grand Prix, Magny Cours, 5 July 1992: Ayrton Senna retired after colliding with Michael Schumacher; the McLaren MP4/7A was no match for the Williams FW14B.

Senna made sure Mansell never had the room to pass, and he won, his fifth victory at Monaco and his fourth in a row, equalling Graham Hill's record for the race. It was Mansell's tyre change that had given Senna the race, and normal Williams' service was resumed at the French Grand Prix: Mansell first, then Patrese and, in third place, Martin Brundle, Senna's old sparring partner from Formula Three, now partnering Schumacher at Benetton. Senna retired after an accident on Lap 3. So it went on. At the British Grand Prix it was Mansell, Patrese and Brundle again, this time Senna retiring with gearbox problems. At Hockenheim, Mansell won again, equalling Senna's record of eight Grands Prix in a season, but Senna put on a great display of skill to come second.

Mansell could win the World Championship at the Hungarian Grand Prix by coming anywhere in the top three. Patrese took the lead and Senna managed to get past Mansell into second place, as did his team mate Berger. There was a lot at stake and Mansell was content with fourth place for a while before he took Berger, moving up to third. Then Patrese spun off, leaving Senna in the lead with Mansell in second place. Senna won, his first victory of the season and the thirty-fifth in his career, second only to Prost in the history of the World Championship.

It had been a frustrating season for Senna, a point emphasized when in his moment of triumph the World Championship crown had passed to Mansell. He knew he was the best driver and he believed he should have the best car. He chose the Hungarian Grand Prix to ease that frustration by setting off a bombshell in the process of musical chairs, designed not only to demonstrate his commitment to racing, but also to destabilize the negotiations over which of the three top

Hungarian Grand Prix, 16 August 1992: a bittersweet moment. Ayrton Senna won the race in an uncompetitive car, but Nigel Mansell's second place gave him the World Championship.

drivers should drive for Williams in 1993. He briefed James Hunt, the BBC commentator and former World Champion with the exclusive news that he was offering his services to Williams in 1993 for nothing. He knew that Prost was in negotiation with Williams and that Nigel Mansell had still not signed up with Williams for 1993. Mansell was reported to be looking for a fee of around £1 million a race, the going rate, so Frank Williams could hardly ignore an offer from a triple World Champion who would cost the team nothing.

With the title decided, the remainder of the season was dominated by politics rather than racing. Schumacher had a maiden victory in Belgium, proof that a third team and new drivers were knocking on the door of the exclusive club. Senna won the Italian Grand Prix and, as the teams were preparing for the Portuguese Grand Prix at Estoril, still nothing was decided about who would drive for Williams, at least not in public. Then on race morning it was announced that the seat would go to Prost. Mansell won the race, making it nine in a season, breaking Senna's record, but he could not compromise with Williams and had started negotiations to quit Formula One to race in America with Paul Newman's Newman-Haas team.

Alain Prost had been in negotiation with Williams for some time. Following his premature departure from Ferrari, he had opened a dialogue almost immediately, helped by the enormous negotiating power of Williams' two main sponsors, Renault and Elf, both gigantic French companies. The negotiations went on behind closed doors, and even as Mansell was winning the Championship for Williams, Prost's well-laid plans to secure a place in the Williams team were bearing fruit and Senna's offer did not influence the decision. Neither could Mansell change the course of

events, he wanted the No.1 driver status he had enjoyed in 1992, and which had given them the World Championship.

Prost arrived at Estoril to test the Williams after the race. There was little Senna could do, but he believed that Prost had kept him out of the Williams team and let his feelings show at the Estoril press conference: 'I do not accept being vetoed by anyone in the way this has been done. This is supposed to be the World Drivers' Championship. We had two fantastic championships this year and last. In 1989 and 1990 we had two very bad ones; they were the consequence of unbelievable politics and bad behaviour by some people. I think we are now coming back to the same situation. If Prost wants to come back and maybe win another title, he should be sporting. The way he is doing it, he is behaving is like a coward. He has everything laid out for him in 1993. It's like running a 100 metre race with him in running shoes and everybody [else] in lead boots. It's not racing'.

The question on most lips was: if the situation had been reversed, would Senna have let Prost in?

Mansell finished the season as World Champion with 108 points, then left for America and the Indycar Championship. Senna was fourth, behind Patrese and Schumacher, with only 50 points. It was a dismal end to the year, one which saw Honda reducing its commitment to racing. The 'lead boot' which Senna was to drive in 1993 was the MP4/8 powered by the Ford HB V-8, the same engine as in the Benetton, though Benetton remained the chosen team for the latest engines and Ford-works support. McLaren had to buy the engines.

How the mighty had fallen. Senna refused to sign a contract with McLaren. In November, he tested for the Penske Indycar team, then went back to his beach-side home in Brazil to be with his family and to jet ski with his nephew and niece for the northern winter while the motor-racing world prepared for the new season. He was the best racing driver in the world, and he believed that he should be accepted on merit, but he had been elbowed aside, the victim of just those politics which he had once used so effectively to put him in the best team.

The Ford-engined McLarens were 80 bhp less powerful than the Renault-powered Williams. Senna would not sign up for McLaren, but agreed to drive for them on a race-by-race basis. In South Africa the magic flared again as Senna swept into the lead and managed to hold Prost off for twenty-three laps, but finally Prost won and Senna was second. The disadvantage between the two cars was too great; gone were the days when Senna could regularly gain pole position and dominate the race from the front.

He sulked. As the date of the next Grand Prix approached, at Interlagos, he kept his team, the organizers and his own home crowd waiting until the day before qualifying until he decided to take part. No team would have tolerated such behaviour from any other driver; strong testimony to both sides of him, his brilliance as a driver and his obsessive self-centredness.

In front of thousands of his most loyal fans he was third on the grid, behind the two Williams of Prost and Damon Hill and he had had to fight for that position with Schumacher who was fourth. The competitive streak took over as the lights turned green and he was between Prost and Hill. Prost started to pull away, then Hill managed to get past Senna. Then it began to rain, but only on part of the circuit, a nightmare for drivers. Several cars spun off, the

yellow flags came out and during the period when they were supposed to stay in their positions Senna overtook Eric Comas' Larrousse and he had to pay a stop-go penalty.

The weather changed everything. Damon Hill came in for wet weather tyres on Lap 28, Prost staying out for an extra lap. It was a serious error. When Christian Fittipaldi's Minardi spun, Prost came up on him, braked, and aquaplaned off the circuit. The safety car came out and everybody held their position with Hill leading. Then the rain stopped and the drivers went in for dry tyres again. Hill came out of the pits just in the lead, but Senna put on the pressure and managed to get past him to win.

It was a glorious moment for Senna and McLaren, their 100th Grand Prix. In adversity, in bad weather, and at a technical disadvantage, the true brilliance of his driving showed. To round off the day, the legendary

Brazilian first: Ayrton Senna in a typical greeting to his most dedicated fans in the city he came from, Sao Paulo; this was his second victory in Brazil.

Argentinian driver, Juan Manuel Fangio, five times
World Champion in the 1950s and now 82 years old,
came to congratulate him. Senna had never made any
secret of his hero worship of Fangio, and that his
greatest dream, having won the World Championship,
was to win it five times like Fangio. They embraced on
the podium and Senna asked if the legendary driver
would present the World Championship trophy to him
should he win it five times. That evening there was a
great party in Sao Paulo.

In the next race he showed why he was rightly
ranked with men like Fangio. The European Grand
Prix was held in Britain, at Donington, the first time a
Grand Prix had been held there since before the war. It
was a grand occasion with King Hussein of Jordan and
the Princess of Wales in attendance with her two sons.
It was a very wet weekend. The Williams were still the
favourites and they were on the front row of the grid,
and Schumacher had managed to pip Senna for third
place this time. Senna had decided to go for Williams
from the off, to use shock tactics before they had time
to settle down. The Williams got away cleanly, but
Schumacher began to edge Senna towards the left,
leaving space on the right of the circuit which Karl
Wendlinger used to good effect to take third place in
his Sauber-Mercedes.

Schumacher beat Senna into the first corner,
putting him fifth, but Senna was fired up, and he put
every last ounce of skill and nerve into the next
minute. As Schumacher accelerated out of the first
corner, he found Senna passing him on the inside. On
the next, he took Wendlinger on the outside, then, in
the space of two more corners, he took Hill. Prost was
a little more difficult, but coming into the Melbourne
Hairpin, Senna took the inside line and scrambled past,

*European Grand
Prix, Donington,
11 April 1993:
Ayrton Senna's
finest moment,
taking his arch
rival, Alain Prost,
on Lap 1 having
started out in
fifth place.*

crossing the line in first place at the end of the first lap. Those in the grandstands and the pits looked on in disbelief; they knew they had seen an historic moment.

Once in front he stayed there, through numerous tyre changes, driving not only at the limit but driving a brilliant tactical race. Once again, adversity had brought out the best in his driving and in the view of many, it was his finest race. The first lap will endure in the history books alongside the all-time great moments in the sport of motor-racing.

At the press conference, Prost was understandably gloomy. He had joined Williams because they had the best car and he had won the first race of the season. Now, with three races run, Senna was 12 points ahead of him in the Championship, in a car which was supposedly no match for the Williams. Senna was clearly delighted. When Prost talked about problems with his car on the first lap, Senna responded with an irony that was lost on nobody: 'Maybe he should change cars with me.'

Senna then let his frustrations out in public again. He was 22 points ahead of the Benetton driver, Michael Schumacher, and Benetton was getting Ford's 'premium' engines. Senna wanted the best engines and he said so, pointing out that Ford had no hope of winning the Championship with any other driver, so why not back him. The small matter of a contractual arrangement between Ford and Benetton seemed a minor matter to him.

He retired at Imola with hydraulic failure, came second to Prost in Spain, where, in a rare moment of fraternity, they shook hands again. Senna won Monaco for the sixth time, beating Graham Hill's record. By a combination of sheer artistry in driving, backed up with the cunning of a street fighter when he needed it,

he just kept his World Championship lead after six races with 42 points to Prost's 37.

Senna was still deeply frustrated that the McLaren was not competitive, but before the French Grand Prix he committed to the McLaren team for the rest of the season. Even as he did so, his Championship hopes were beginning to fade. Prost won the Canadian, French, British and German Grands Prix, taking back the lead in the Championship. At Silverstone, Senna led, then tried intimidating Prost whenever he came alongside to overtake, making sudden moves towards the Williams, but Prost found a way through. At Hockenheim when they disputed the chicane on the first lap, Prost would not give way and Senna lost control and spun off. It seemed that nothing in his reserves of skill and nerve could make up for the difference in performance of the cars and for a time Senna's motivation seemed to flag.

Towards the end of the season that changed. Once Prost had won the title in Portugal, he announced his retirement, leaving the Williams seat free. With Mansell still in America, where he had won the Indycar Championship, it seemed that it was Senna's turn to go to Williams. He had made it plain that he would not be staying at McLaren unless they could find a more powerful engine, and when the opportunity arose at Williams he took it.

The future assured, Senna the supreme driver was in evidence again. At Suzuka, scene of some of his best drives and also of his most notable controversies with Prost, they were alongside each other on the front row of the grid. Prost was on pole, but Senna made the better start and was leading by 2 seconds at the end of the first lap. Senna pitted early for tyres, giving Prost the lead. Then it rained. Both drivers were on slicks and Senna passed Prost just before they both went in for wets. Prost had a very bad pit stop, rejoining 25 seconds behind Senna. Then Senna came to Damon Hill and the Ulsterman, Eddie Irvine, driving for Jordan-Hart in his first ever Grand Prix. Irvine did not observe the customary swift move to let Senna through, but went on battling with Hill, sliding up on to the grass and showering Senna's McLaren with dirt and stones. Senna got past Irvine, but before he could take Hill, Irvine repassed him; Senna eventually passed them both.

Prost could not make up the difference and Senna won his fortieth Grand Prix, simultaneously taking McLaren's total to 103, equalling Ferrari's all-time record. It should have been a day of celebration, but Senna was furious with Irvine and could not let it drop. First, he rounded on Irvine in the press conference, saying: 'He shouldn't be driving in Formula One if he can't respect other drivers. He carried on like he didn't give a damn about anybody else. His attitude was screw them all.'

Not content with that, Senna went round to the Jordan pits and confronted Irvine who was completely unrepentant. This infuriated Senna even more. In a torrent of abuse and a few threats, Senna tried to humiliate Irvine shouting: 'You're not a racing driver, you're a f*****g idiot.'

The real problem was that Irvine had not shown the respect that Senna demanded, either on the track or in the pits and he knew he was not getting through to Irvine. He turned to go, then in a moment of rage, he turned back and hit Irvine on the side of the head. Jordan lodged an official complaint.

Irvine, for whom Senna had been a hero on his own way up through the lower formulas, had seen at first hand the obsessive and selfish side in Senna and he was frank about it: 'I think he's got a serious problem. He thinks he's God's gift to racing drivers. Its his game of marbles and he wants to keep all the marbles.'

On another occasion, when it was pointed out to Ayrton Senna that he had been known to hinder other drivers who wanted to overtake he responded: 'But I am Senna.'

The final race of the season was in Adelaide, Australia. With Alain Prost retiring, it was clearly going to be the final confrontation between Senna and Prost, but the mood was of celebration and goodwill. Prost was the most successful driver in the history of Grand Prix racing and Senna, still regarded by many as the most talented driver in the sport, if not of all time, was the only man who could possibly hope to emulate his record in the years to come.

It was vintage Senna. He took pole position, led the race from start to finish, save for pit stops, and Prost was second by 9 seconds. McLaren had beaten Ferrari's record by one Grand Prix to become the highest scoring team in the history of the sport, many of them down to the two drivers who were indulging in a display of back-slapping and hugging on the podium which must have brought ironic tears to a great many eyes.

They had been the master drivers of the high-technology age of motor racing. Between them, they had won the Drivers' Championship seven times in ten years, six times for McLaren. These had been years of seemingly limitless money which paid for the technology and the drivers' fees, and Senna and Prost epitomized the glamour which global interest in Formula One had brought, along with commercialism and earnings on a scale no other sport could match.

Australian Grand Prix, 7 November 1993: Ayton Senna celebrates his last Grand Prix victory.

One of them was going and one of them was staying, but Adelaide 1993 was truly the end of an era.

For 1994 the FIA had changed the rules, taking away much of the high-tech, the computers and the driver aids in favour of simpler cars. The aim was to encourage more competition between drivers rather than between money and computers. Williams was on top and a new season stretched ahead, full of promise. The Senna-Williams combination seemed to meet the ideal again – the world's fastest driver in the fastest Formula One car. But the shifting sands of politics had not been still in the off-season, and it was soon clear in testing that the fairy tale was not necessarily going to happen; the combination of Benetton-Ford and Michael Schumacher was growing in technical prowess and confidence and Schumacher was seen as the new challenger for the Championship even before the first race.

At Interlagos, in front of that fervent home crowd for the eleventh time, Ayrton Senna spun off while chasing Schumacher. No other car was involved. In the Pacific Grand Prix in Japan, he was on pole position. When Senna and Schumacher arrived at the first corner, Schumacher was just in the lead. Mika Hakkinen was right on Senna's gearbox, and when he was forced to lift off slightly, Hakkinen's McLaren touched the back of Senna's car, causing him to spin off. The third race of 1994 was at Imola on May Day.

In the weeks that followed Ayrton Senna's death, it was like a family closing ranks; difficult relationships were set aside and sometimes bitter rows forgotten in Formula One's spasm of collective grief. Only those members close to the heart of it understood. Ron Dennis was at the heart of that family and that is how he described it in an interview with *Motoring News* a

month later: 'When Ayrton lost his life, it was like losing your own child … if you love the family, you have to be able to rise above those day-to-day values and say: "Right, we're family. It doesn't matter that he's a black sheep, she's a withering granny who's a little senile; the family's got to come first".'

It was a sentiment and an analogy which Ayrton Senna would have understood. So would Alain Prost, who was shattered: 'The only driver I respected…with his death, half my career has gone.'

'The greatest driver ever,' said Niki Lauda, one of the foremost campaigners for safety, 'when someone like him is killed you have to ask yourself what is the point of it all.' Jackie Stewart said of Senna : 'Senna was one of the greatest talents. This has totally shocked the racing community.'

'Fearless, highly talented and also highly intelligent … probably the best all-round driver that's ever existed,' said Ron Dennis. Frank Williams, whose branch of the family Senna had moved to only months before, but who had known him for more than a decade, since he gave him a test for Formula One: 'Everyone who has ever met him in whatever capacity feels they have lost someone very special.'

In Argentina, Juan Manuel Fangio grieved for Senna: 'I cannot get this accident out of my head, the accident to one whom I believe to be the worthiest of my successors as World Champion, the only one capable of surpassing my record of five world titles.'

BBC commentator Murray Walker called him: 'Arguably the greatest racing driver who ever lived.'

It was a sentiment echoed again and again in the summer of 1994 in the hundreds of news bulletins and acres of newsprint which marked Senna's death. The idea of the greatest driver to have raced was a simple, direct and instant way of encapsulating a talented and complex man in a single idea which expressed, too, the enormity of the loss. It is impossible to make an objective judgement across hundreds of top drivers over a century, but comparing drivers is one way, probably the only way, of trying to put Ayrton Senna into some kind of historical perspective.

In a contemporary sense the most obvious is Alain Prost, Senna's greatest rival, though Prost's career was longer. Because they were contemporaries and drove cars which were broadly similar, sometimes identical, the statistics are interesting. Prost won four World Championships to Senna's three, but that was in a career of thirteen years to Senna's ten making them broadly equal. With fifty-one victories Prost won more Grands Prix than Senna with forty-one, but Prost also drove in many more races, 199 to Senna's 161. Crude mathematics shows that taking their victories as a percentage of races driven, their performance was virtually identical with Senna just a whisker ahead: Prost 25.62% to Senna's 25.94%. But a similar exercise with pole positions, no bad measure of pure driving ability, has Senna way ahead with sixty-two giving him 39.24% to Prost's thirty-two amounting to only 16.08%.

Such comparisons are interesting only, they do not prove anything other than what we already know, namely that when Senna and Prost raced each other they were very closely fought. In the years they were both at McLaren, 1988 and 1989, they each took a title.

Going back into history, the most frequent comparison has been with Jim Clark. Statistics are completely meaningless across thirty years, so much has changed, so we are thrown back on memory, and on looking at a range of qualities.

Jim Clark: started in seventy-two Grands Prix of which he won twenty-five, taking thirty-three pole positions and two World Championships in 1963 and 1965, before his death in 1968.

Clark only ever drove for one team, Lotus, and together they were dominant, just as Senna and Prost were with McLaren. Chapman put together the ideal combination of car, engine and driver in the 1960s, just as Ron Dennis did in 1988. If anything, Clark appeared to dominate more in the mid-1960s than Senna did because there was no Prost equivalent in the team. The sense of excitement at a race in which Clark was driving was palpable. From anywhere in the grandstand or round the circuit, you knew where he was and you waited for some sublime piece of driving or thrilling manoeuvre effortlessly executed. Senna had that quality, that presence on the circuit which no other driver of the last ten years could match. The sad fact is that it is in the manner of their deaths that they are so close, both dying at the wheel at the peak of their careers, with a great deal behind them and a great deal ahead of them, too, carrying the hopes and dreams of the entire sport on their shoulders.

Making historical comparisons between drivers is a minefield, but four beg to be made because they share a common theme with Senna across many years. Sometimes, when the best driver is not driving the best car, he can still win. On some occasions it has been down to skill alone, brilliant driving triumphing

over technical disadvantage, and when that happens it goes into the history books.

In 1935, Tazio Nuvolari, somebody of whom it has often been said was the greatest driver of all time, wanted to join the mighty German Auto Union team. He was kept out partly because he was of low birth, and partly because his great rival, Achille Varzi, had got into the team first and blocked him. At the German Grand Prix at the Nurburgring, the two great

Tazio Nuvolari's career lasted from 1921 to 1948; in 1993, he was voted the greatest driver in the history of the sport in a debate at Britain's National Motor Museum.

German teams, Auto Union and Mercedes were out in force, massively backed by both commercial and Nazi propaganda funds. The top drivers were all there competing for the 'Adolf Hitler Preis': Rudolf Caracciola, Manfred von Brauchitsch and Luigi Fagioli and for Auto Union, Varzi, Bernd Rosemeyer and Hans Stuck, every one of them in the exclusive club of top drivers, or about to be. Nuvolari turned up in an obsolete Alfa Romeo P.3, a great car in its day, but its days were over. It had been bored out and tuned to give him 330 bhp, but that was still 100 bhp below the 430 bhp of the Mercedes W25Bs. In front of a highly partisan crowd, Nuvolari picked off the cream of the most powerful teams of their day, or they retired, or he pressurized them into making mistakes.

In 1936, Rudolf Caracciola, one of the drivers whom Nuvolari beat at the Nurbergring, drove to

Rudolf Caracciola: the original 'Regenmeister' and star Mercedes driver of the 1930s; he won twenty-six major Grand Prix and was European Champion in 1935, 1937 and 1938.

victory at Monaco in torrential rain on a surface covered in oil. There were spins and collisions all through the race, but Caracciola demonstrated an uncanny level of control in the wet which earned him the title 'Regenmeister', master of the rain, a tribute to his ability to control his car and stay competitive in even the most slippery conditions.

In 1957, again at the Nurburgring, the German Grand Prix was a battle between Juan Manuel Fangio, aged 46, who needed to win it to clinch his fifth World Championship. He was driving a Maserati 250F, one of the classic racing cars of all time, but nearing the end of its life. Against him were Mike Hawthorn and Peter Collins, both in the latest Ferraris. They could carry enough fuel for the whole race, while Fangio would have to stop once. He started with only half a tank, planning to build up a sufficient lead while he was light, to enable him to stop and rejoin the race in the lead. All went according to plan, and he was leading by 30 seconds when he made the pit stop on Lap 12. It went disastrously wrong, and he rejoined the race 45 seconds behind the two Ferraris. Undaunted, he set out after them driving to the limit, sharing an experience which Senna encountered at Monaco in 1984, where he was transported into a state of concentration which let him go over the limit. He broke his own lap record several times, astonishing the timekeepers and the two Ferrari drivers as he took them to win by 3.6 seconds, saying at the end of it: 'I did things I have never done before and I do not ever want to do again.'

The fourth race is the 1961 Monaco Grand Prix. The formula had just been changed and Ferrari was well prepared with a new engine, but the British engine manufacturer, Coventry Climax, had not

Juan Manuel Fangio (right), five times World Champion, 1951, 1954, 1955, 1956, and 1957, with Stirling Moss, the greatest driver never to take the title.

brought out a new engine, so Lotus and Cooper were using whatever they could find. Stirling Moss was driving an obsolete car, a Lotus 18, with a Formula Two engine. He was up against a Ferrari team of Phil Hill, the reigning World Champion, Ritchie Ginther and Wolfgang von Trips. Moss took pole position, but the Ferraris led at the start. He managed to get past them on Lap 14, and pulled slightly ahead. They fought back, and for the rest of the race there was barely 11 seconds covering the first three cars. But each time the red cars moved up on him, Moss found a reserve of speed or judgement which kept him ahead.

These are stories of classic drives, not classic cars, of races won by drivers on rare talent alone, not by men in superior cars, but by men against superior cars which made their task look impossible. Senna's victory at Donington in 1993 was just such a race and, with many others, puts Ayrton Senna on a par with the greatest names in the history of the sport, Nuvolari, Caracciola, Fangio, Moss and Clark.

As a driver, Ayrton Senna's place in the history of the sport is unassailable, but as a sportsman and as an individual, his position is much less well defined. One summing up is that he was widely respected for his driving talent, but that he was not well liked. He was aware of that and it barely troubled him; he considered it to be all part of the job. In a BBC documentary made in 1993 he said: 'Its no good to be nice, to take it easy, because if you are going to be nice and take it easy you might as well do something else, stay home or have an ordinary profession. Being in a competitive environment, and a very tough one, you have to be tough. You have to be hard, sometimes you can be a little too hard, but better to be on the harder side than on the easy one.'

He did not shrink from using intimidation to win, and he knew the psychological pressure it put on other drivers: not backing off and waiting for his opponent to do so instead was all part of being a legend, part of the psychological battle before and during the race. His hardness, his arrogance, his aggressiveness, his selfishness, his aloofness and his combativeness made him a difficult man to deal with and a more controversial figure than any other in the sport. Any sport is about winning, but it is also about taking part, being part of the sport as a whole, something Senna never did easily. He was one of the architects, one of the arbiters and one of the products of the modern age of professional sporting heroes, for whom winning is all: 'The most important thing for me is to win. The few seconds of pleasure I get when I overtake or gain a pole position or win a race is my motivation.'

Of less, but only slightly less, importance was money, not so much for its own sake, as for the way it represented winning. Formula One is secretive about

Brazilian Grand
Prix, Interlagos,
28 March 1993:
head to head with
Damon Hill,
Ayrton Senna
passes Hill in
the superior
Williams to win
for Brazil.

money, but around $25–$30 million is the going rate for a driver and though he once offered to drive for Frank Williams for nothing, that was a ploy to put him in a winning team: 'At the end you get paid what you're worth. If you get paid one dollar or a million dollars, its because its what you can offer back.'

Once at a press conference he was asked whether he helped the street children of his home town of Sao Paulo: 'I do. Don't ask any more.' He did, but his charitable work and donations were, like his private life, shrouded in secrecy and linked with his religious faith. He once explained why he kept his charity secret: 'I do this because I believe in it and other people and the media may choose to suggest other reasons which are irrelevant.'

After his death some details of his charity donations emerged. Carlos Alberto Lancelotti of the Assistencia da Crianca Defeituosa (The Charity for Disabled Children) in Sao Paulo revealed that he had made a single donation of $100,000 which was used for a hospital which now treats 720 people a day, most of them children. He donated $75,000 to a fund for medical assistance to rubber extractors and Indians in the Acre, in the Amazon region, and once paid $65,000 for a life-saving operation for a young girl whose family had no money.

He could easily be touched and there was a very soft side to his character. Reports of tears in his eyes when he won races, or when he was faced with huge pressures, fill reports of his career. Sometimes they were tears of frustration, at not getting his own way. More often they were tears brought on by the release of bottled-up emotion, such was the level of control which he exerted over his mind in the build up to a race. Sometimes he cried because he felt he had been

Testing for Williams in Portugal. Motor racing was one hundred years old in 1994, and for ten years Ayrton Senna was the most talented and exciting driver to reach the top of the sport.

unjustly treated, but the tears in his eyes at Imola when he heard about the death of Roland Ratzenberger and when he went to visit Rubens Barrichello in hospital after his accident the day before, were nothing to do with racing; the young driver was his protégé, a brother nearly lost, another boy from Brazil, from Sao Paulo, somebody who was making his way. Barrichello was one of his few friends among Formula One drivers: 'Most of my friends are from five to ten years ago. I don't have new friends, but I get on well with the young people of Formula One.'

His relationships with women were very public, being photographed with them at events, but the details remained very private. On television he would talk about racing but he did not go in for the exposure of his emotional life as so many global stars of screen and sports field have done. Few of his relationships with women have lasted longer than a year or so, and though he spoke of needing a partner in life, there is no evidence that he intended to do so while he was still racing. His deepest emotional life was with his close family, especially with his sister Viviane's children.

The two sides of Ayrton Senna – the popular hero driven to win at all costs, and the caring, intelligent private man – coexisted comfortably for him. For those around him it was more difficult.

He could have been successful in many walks of life and found his way to the top, but he chose the demanding, competitive world of motor racing. He made mistakes, but his judgement was more often spot on; he understood clearly what was needed to get to the top, and applied himself to it. Motor racing shaped his life, more than that, it took over his life.

Ayrton Senna would not have been Ayrton Senna without motor racing. He was selfish, a born winner, outwardly secure to the point of arrogance and, coolly confident of winning. But without that profound and often irritating self-belief, he would not have been the winner he was and that is what motor racing is all about.

His position as the leading driver in the Formula One World Championship has already been assumed by Michael Schumacher. The show must go on: Ayrton Senna will be replaced on the circuit, and to an extent in the grandstands and on television where billions of fans watched the sport because when he was racing they never knew quite what to expect. Ayrton Senna will inevitably be missed less and less, but he will never be forgotten by those who saw him drive and those who saw him win.

Dream drive: Ayrton Senna finally gets to grips with the fabulous Williams FW16 in preparation for his eleventh season in Formula One.

CHAPTER SEVEN

CAREER RECORD

AYRTON SENNA
21.03.60 - 01.05.94

GRAND PRIX STARTS: 161
GRAND PRIX POLE POSITIONS: 65
GRAND PRIX FASTEST LAPS: 19
GRAND PRIX WINS: 41

WORLD CHAMPIONSHIP

1984	9th	13 pts

(equal with Nigel Mansell)

1985	4th	38 pts
1986	4th	55 pts
1987	3rd	57 pts
1988	1st	90 pts

First World Championship

1989	2nd	60 pts
1990	1st	78 pts

Second World Championship

1991	1st	96 pts

Third World Championship

1992	4th	50 pts
1993	2nd	73 pts

Records: 13 pole positions in one season – 1988

1973

1 July – Kart Race, Interlagos – 1st. Ayrton Senna da Silva's first competitive race, which he won.

1977

South American Kart Champion

1978

South American Kart Champion
Brazilian Kart Champion
World Kart Championships
Le Mans, France,
13-17 September – 6th.

1979

Brazilian Kart Champion
World Kart Championships
Estoril, Portugal,
18-23 September – 2nd.

1980

Brazilian Kart Champion
World Kart Championships
Nivelles, Belgium,
17-21 September – 2nd.

1981

Brazilian Kart Champion
Van Diemen RF80-Ford

1 March – P & O Championship – Brands Hatch

Ayrton Senna's first race in Britain. Having risen to fourth place, he was overtaken by fellow Van Diemen driver, Mexican Alfonso Toledano, to finish 5th.

Van Diemen RF81-Ford

8 March – Townsend Thoresen Championship (TT) – Thruxton

Senna was involved in a tussle with Argentinian driver Enrique Mansilla but eventually escaped from the pack. Royale-Nelson team drivers Rick Morris and David Wheeler dominated the race, but when Mansilla headed for the pits, Senna held on to 3rd against a challenge from Toledano.

15 March – TT – Brands Hatch

In the pouring rain, Senna won the first heat against a strong challenge from Mansilla. In the final he held off challenges from Andy Ackerley, who spun off trying to outbrake Senna, and Steve Lincoln, to win his first Formula Ford 1600 race by 15 seconds.

22 March – TT – Mallory

Senna took his first pole position but was beaten at the start by Mansilla. After beating off challenges from Ricardo Valerio, Alfonso Toledano and Rick Morris, he pursued Mansilla and on the last lap was edged on to the grass when he tried to overtake. There was an angry altercation with Mansilla afterwards.

5 April – TT – Mallory

Toledano took pole position with Senna 2nd on the grid. He and Toledano jostled all the way, and Senna took the lead on Lap 4. But with three laps to go, Rick Morris sneaked through as the two Van Diemen drivers 'fell over each other' at Shaws. Morris won from Senna by 0.2 seconds.

3 May – TT – Snetterton

Senna took pole position and won in the rain. Afterwards he was spotted by Dennis Rushen who offered him a Formula Ford 2000 drive for 1982, which Senna later accepted.

24 May – Royal Automobile Club (RAC) Championship – Oulton Park

Senna equalled the two-year-old lap record to qualify in pole position. Toledano emerged as leader after the first corner, with Senna 2nd, but Senna overtook him on the next lap and took the fastest lap, to win from Morris by 1.7 seconds.

25 May – TT – Mallory

Senna made a good start and dominated the race, winning by 6 seconds from Morris.

7 June – TT – Snetterton

Senna dominated the seventh round of the TT Championship with Morris 2nd; he recorded the fastest lap.

21 June – RAC – Silverstone

A classic race in which Senna got a good start and took the lead but was caught by Morris on Lap 5. Morris spent the rest of the race working out how to overtake Senna, passing him on the final lap, only to be passed by Senna almost immediately. Senna clung to the outside line and at the final chicane Morris bounced his car over the kerbs, scraping past to put Senna 2nd, making them level on points in the RAC Championship.

27 June – TT – Oulton Park

In practice Senna beat the long-standing lap record by 0.1 seconds, a time equalled by Morris. But Morris retired on Lap 2 after which Senna dominated, also taking the fastest lap.

4 July – RAC – Donington

Senna took the lead in the RAC Championship, winning and taking fastest lap despite a strong challenge from Morris who started to close in the final laps.

12 July – RAC – Brands Hatch

Senna started on the third row of the grid after problems getting the car set up, but he made a sensational start and overtook four cars to take the lead on the first lap. With three laps to go the car slewed sideways and he rejoined in 4th place with a water hose adrift; he finished 4th with fastest lap.

25 July – TT – Oulton Park

Senna shared the front row with team mate Toledano and another Brazilian, Fernando Macedo. Toledano took the lead but Senna passed him on the first lap and again won impressively with fastest lap.

26 July – RAC – Mallory

Senna took pole position and won, while Morris, Toledano and Mansilla fought for 2nd place; Senna also took fastest lap.

2 August – TT – Brands Hatch

Senna stormed into the lead on Lap 1 and held it for the rest of the race while Morris and Toledano fought for 2nd. After ten of the thirteen rounds of the TT, Senna had 183 points to Morris's 136.

9 August – RAC – Snetterton
Toledano led at the end of Lap 1, followed by Senna and Mansilla; Senna passed him, equalling the long standing lap record, and when it began to rain took out a 2 second advantage over him; by winning he became RAC Champion.

15 August – EDFA Euroseries – Donington
Senna stormed into the lead, winning his eleventh Formula Ford 1600 race from eighteen starts.

31 August – TT – Thruxton
Senna took pole position by 0.5 seconds. By Lap 3 he had established firm control and won comfortably, with the fastest lap. He clinched the Townsend Thoresen Championship, the first Brazilian to win two titles in a year.

16-20 September – World Kart Championships – Parma, Italy
Senna came 4th.

29 September – TT – Brands Hatch
Senna was pushed down the running order by two incidents on the first lap, but drove brilliantly to finish 2nd; he also took fastest lap by 1 second.

1982
Formula Ford 2000 (Rushen Green Racing)
Pace British (PB) & European 2000 (EFDA)
Driving Van Diemen RF82-Ford

7 March – PB – Brands Hatch
Senna took pole position by 0.6 seconds in his first Formula Ford 2000 race, establishing a 60-yard lead half way round the first lap; he won his first Formula Ford 2000 race by 14 seconds.

27 March – PB – Oulton
Senna took pole position, went into the lead and was never caught; he also set a new lap record by 0.2 seconds to maintain full points in the Pace British Championship.

28 March – PB – Silverstone
Senna took pole position and broke the lap record, winning by 17 seconds from Colin Jack's Reynard.

4 April – PB – Donington
Senna took pole position, fastest lap and scored his fourth successive Formula Ford 2000 victory.

9 April – PB – Snetterton
Senna took pole position and went into the lead, but was slowed by the wreckage of a first-corner crash. He was overtaken by fellow Van Diemen drivers Andrews and Spence, lost his front breaks, then regained the lead to win his fifth race in a row; he also took fastest lap.

12 April – PB – Silverstone
Senna took pole position, equalled his own lap record, and was never challenged. He was offered contracts with Toleman and McLaren but turned them down.

18 April – EFDA – Zolder
Senna took pole position in the first race of the European Formula Ford 2000 Championship. It should have been a classic confrontation between Senna and Cor Euser – European, Dutch and Benelux Formula Ford 1600 Champion – but delays at the start led Senna's engine to overheat and after taking the lead, he retired on Lap 2.

2 May – EFDA – Donington
In the second Euroseries race Senna took pole position and broke his own lap record by 0.11 seconds; he won by 7 seconds from Spence with Euser 5th.

3 May – PB – Mallory

Senna's engine was down on power in qualifying and he was beaten to pole position by Victor Rosso. Rosso fluffed his start and Senna went into the lead to win by 8 seconds, also taking fastest lap.

9 May – EFDA – Zolder

In the third round of the Euroseries, Senna took pole position and fastest lap, but in a rare error spun off into the catch-fencing, throwing away an almost certain victory.

30 May – PB – Oulton Park

Senna's engine was down on power and Calvin Fish took pole position in a new Van Diemen RF82. Fish took the lead and Senna, struggling with a punctured tyre, was overtaken by Kenny Andrews, Neil Myers and Tim Davies. After sliding several times, Senna's rear right tyre exploded at 125 mph but he managed to steer the car to safety.

30 May – Shell Sunbeam Celebrity Race – Oulton Park

Driving Sunbeam Talbot T1, Senna set a new class lap record and won by 7 seconds.

31 May – PB – Brands Hatch

Calvin Fish again took pole position; Senna, however, took the lead on the first lap and fought off a challenge from Fish to win by 2 seconds, also taking fastest lap.

6 June – PB – Mallory

In the tenth round of the PB Championship, Senna again failed to take pole position, which went to Tim Davies. But Senna quickly took the lead and won by 15 seconds, with fastest lap.

13 June – PB – Brands Hatch

Senna took pole position and led from the start. But he was followed all the way by Calvin Fish, whom he beat by 1 second. During their duel Senna set a new lap record, which was later equalled by Fish.

20 June – EFDA – Hockenheim

In the fourth round of the Euroseries Senna took pole position but cooked his clutch on the start-line; Euser led the race and Senna crashed at the first chicane.

26 June – PB – Oulton Park

Senna was beaten by Kenny Andrews on the opening lap but gained the lead on the second lap and held it for the rest of the race, taking fastest lap; he won by 4 seconds from Calvin Fish.

3 July – EFDA – Zandvoort

In the fifth round of the EFDA, Senna missed the first practice session with a clutch problem, but he still took pole position. On the first lap he missed second gear allowing Jaap van Silfhout to take the lead, but passed him on the second lap and won by 2 seconds from Calvin Fish; it was Senna's first victory in Europe but second in the series.

4 July – PB – Snetterton

Tyres were the deciding factor at the Snetterton track, which was still wet but drying quickly. Having fought a battle with Calvin Fish for much of the race, Senna got past him but was caught by Frank Bradley on the final lap, Bradley being the only driver to have opted for slicks; Senna said afterwards 'He was the best today.'

10 July – PB – Castle Combe

Senna took pole position and broke the lap record by 0.9 seconds; having led the race from the start he won by 3 seconds from Fish.

1 August – PB – Snetterton

Senna and Fish were on the front row of the grid; Senna took the lead but by Lap 4, Fish was challenging. As Fish tried to pass him on the

Revitt straight Senna pushed him on to the grass and Fish retired, angry; Senna won. After the race, Fish reported Senna who was fined £200 but allowed to keep his points.

8 August – EFDA – Hockenheim

The sixth round of the European Championship: Senna took pole position by 3 seconds and soon established himself in the lead; he won having again taken fastest lap.

15 August – EFDA – Osterreichring

The seventh round of the European Championship: Senna took pole position, fastest lap, and won by a staggering 24 seconds over Fish.

22 August – EFDA – Jyllandsring, Denmark

Senna took pole position, broke the lap record and won, taking the European Formula Ford 2000 Championship in addition to the British Championship.

30 August – PB – Thruxton

Fish took pole position by 0.3 seconds from Senna and took the lead with Senna chasing. On Lap 4 Senna's car developed oil pressure problems and he wasn't able to overtake Fish until Lap 13, with oil smoke pouring from his engine. He won, and broke the lap record.

5 September – PB – Silverstone

Senna and Fish recorded identical times in practice and jointly posted fastest lap; Senna immediately took the lead and won, despite a race-long challenge from Fish.

12 September – B & H Leinster Trophy RAC – Mondello Park

In the pre-race Irish round, Senna was second for the first two laps behind Irishman Joey Greenan, but was soon in the lead and smashed the lap record. In the 'final' Greenan got away first again, but was soon overtaken by Senna who won by over 20 seconds.

15-19 September – World Kart Championships – Kalmar, Sweden

Senna was 14th after a disastrous Championship.

26 September – PB – Brands Hatch

In the final race, Senna only qualified on the second row of the grid. Fish took the lead and Senna overtook Rosso to take 2nd place, but was unable to catch Fish.

Driving Ralt RT3-Toyota

13 November – Formula Three, non-championship race – Thruxton

In his first Formula Three race, Senna took pole position and broke the lap record set by Dave Scott. He finished 13 seconds ahead of Swede Bengt Tragardh and later signed for Formula Three with Dick Bennetts' West Surrey Racing.

1983
Marlboro British Formula Three Championship (West Surrey Racing) – Ralt RT3-Toyota

6 March – Silverstone

In his first Formula Three Championship race Senna qualified in 2nd position behind David Leslie; he took the lead on the first corner and won by 7 seconds from Martin Brundle.

13 March – Thruxton

Senna took pole position and, after a wheel-to-wheel skirmish with Brundle on Lap 1, emerged in front. While Senna was faster through the corners, Brundle outpaced him on the straights. Senna stayed just ahead of Brundle to win, also taking fastest lap.

Formula 3, 1983

20 March – Silverstone

Senna took pole position and went straight into the lead; at Becketts, Brundle got past as Senna went wide, but Senna went past on the outside at Stowe, a manoeuvre which Brundle later described as 'quite brilliant'. Later, after a restart, Brundle got away quicker but Senna again got past on the outside. On the final lap Senna's fire extinguisher went off but he was unflustered, taking his fourth straight victory and the fastest lap.

27 March – Donington

Senna, recently celebrating his twenty-third birthday, took pole position and went into the lead. By Lap 4 he was 2 seconds ahead and he won the race by 5 seconds, breaking the lap record. *Autosport* asked 'Is Ayrton Senna da Silva really invincible?'

4 April – Thruxton

'Why doesn't he make any mistakes?' asked Martin Brundle dolefully afterwards, but Senna had made a rare error at the start after taking pole position. He missed second gear, allowing American Davy Jones and Brundle to get past; Jones led for two laps before Senna passed for his sixth successive win.

24 April – Silverstone

Senna took pole position, fastest lap and led throughout, while Jones and Brundle fought it out for second place; Senna now had 58 points to Brundle's 38 in the Championship.

2 May – Thruxton

Senna took pole position and fastest lap in a by now familiar race formation: Senna – Brundle – Jones; it was his seventh straight win.

8 May – Brands Hatch

Senna took pole position in a torrential rain storm, then led to the finish: Senna – Brundle – Jones. He declared it his best win yet.

30 May – Silverstone

Senna took pole position and fastest lap, winning his tenth straight Formula Three race in a row, with Brundle behind as usual.

12 June – European Formula Three Trophy Race – Silverstone

In the first round of the European Championship, Martin Brundle finally broke Senna's run, taking pole position. Brundle got off into the lead. Senna gambled on three different types of tyres, a policy which failed; on Lap 6 he spun off spectacularly, rejoining in 9th place. On Lap 8 his car flew backwards into the catch fencing and failed to finish the race, the first time that season.

19 June – Cadwell Park

After smashing Enrique Mansilla's year-old lap record, and with 2 minutes of qualifying left, Senna strayed wide on to the grass, exiting the right-hander; he crashed heavily and was out of the race; Brundle won.

3 July – Snetterton

Senna could only qualify fourth, to his puzzlement and that of Dick Bennetts. When Brundle, on pole, took the lead, Senna chased him all the way; on Lap 24, of twenty-five, Brundle forced Senna off the track as Senna tried to take the inside line and his wheel ran up over Brundle's, causing him to crash; Senna lodged a complaint against Brundle, but to no avail; it was the third race he had failed to finish.

16 July – Silverstone

Senna took pole position from Brundle by 0.04 seconds and held the lead by a narrow margin all the way to the finish; he also took fastest lap.

24 July – Donington

Senna took pole position and fastest lap, but for the first time was beaten into 2nd place by Brundle who took the lead on the first lap and drove a superlative race to win by 0.4 seconds.

6 August – Oulton Park

The Senna-Brundle battle hotted up as Brundle managed to beat Senna in qualifying taking pole. Brundle then took the lead and held it until on Lap 28 when Senna, after setting fastest lap, ran up the back of him and both cars retired. Most observers put the blame firmly on Senna who was fined and his licence was endorsed.

29 August – Silverstone

Senna took pole and never looked like being caught by Brundle; it was his eleventh win of the year.

11 September – Oulton Park

Senna took pole position but lost the lead to Brundle and crashed and retired when attempting to overtake Brundle on the outside at Druids on Lap 8; Senna was in danger of losing the Championship because as Brundle put it, 'it appears he can't accept finishing second.'

18 September – Thruxton

Senna took pole position but lost the lead to Brundle on the first lap. Senna overtook him, but Brundle re-passed him again on Lap 2; Senna's engine then expired. Brundle won, bringing the gap in the Championship down to 3 points.

2nd October – Silverstone

Senna qualified 4th, but by the end of Lap 1 he and Brundle had moved clear of the rest of the field. After ten laps Brundle was leading by 1.5 seconds, but on the final lap Senna closed and was threatening at Becketts; he then decided to settle for second place; Brundle was 1 point ahead in the Championship with one race to go.

20 October – Formula Three Grand Prix – Macau, Portugal

Senna took pole position, fastest lap and won.

23 October – Thruxton

Senna clinched the British Formula Three Championship in an anti-climactic race which had been billed as the showdown between Senna and Brundle. After taking pole position he went into the lead and after two laps was 2 seconds ahead. Brundle was involved in a scrap for 2nd with Jones, which he eventually lost. Senna also took the fastest lap.

In twenty-one Formula Three races Senna had taken pole sixteen times.

1984
Toleman TG183B-Hart

25 March – Brazilian Grand Prix – Rio de Janeiro

1st Alain Prost – McLaren – TAG
2nd Keke Rosberg – Williams-Honda
3rd Elio de Angelis – Lotus-Renault
In his first Grand Prix, Senna qualified 16th on the grid but retired when his engine lost turbo boost pressure on Lap 8. Prior to the race he made a deal with Brundle that should one of them be noticeably faster the other would not hold him up.

7 April – South African Grand Prix – Kyalami

1st Niki Lauda – McLaren-TAG
2nd Alain Prost– McLaren-TAG
3rd Derek Warwick – Renault
Senna qualified 13th and again experienced boost problems in the early stages. He then hit an object that damaged his nose wings and worsened the already heavy steering. Despite this he finished 6th to earn his first Championship point.

**29 April – Belgian Grand Prix
– Zolder**

1st Michele Alboreto – Ferrari
2nd Derek Warwick – Renault
3rd Rene Arnoux – Ferrari
Senna qualified 19th and finished
7th; his team mate Johnny Cecotto
retired for the third successive race.

**6 May – San Marino Grand
Prix – Imola**

1st Alain Prost – McLaren-TAG
2nd Rene Arnoux – Ferrari
3rd Elio de Angelis – Lotus-Renault
For the only time in his career
Senna failed to qualify. Problems
with Pirelli meant that he did not
get tyres until Saturday and this,
together with a fuel pressure
problem, prevented him from
qualifying.

**12 May – Mercedes–Benz Cup
– Nurburgring**

1st *Ayrton Senna –*
      Mercedes-Benz 190E
2nd Niki Lauda –
      Mercedes-Benz 190E
3rd Carlos Reutemann –
      Mercedes-Benz 190E
At the inaugural race of the new
Nurburgring, Senna won against a
host of champions past and present,
including Moss, Lauda, Reutemann,
Scheckter, Hunt, Surtees and Prost.

Portuguese Grand Prix, 1984

Reutemann was an early leader followed by Alan Jones who retired after three laps. Senna inherited the lead and triumphed despite challenges from Lauda, Watson and Scheckter.

Toleman TG 184–Hart

20 May – French Grand Prix – Dijon-Prenois

1st Niki Lauda – McLaren-TAG
2nd Patrick Tambay – Renault
3rd Nigel Mansell – Lotus-Renault
Driving the new Toleman TG 184, Senna qualified 13th and was lying in ninth place when he retired on Lap 34 with turbo failure.

3 June – Monaco Grand Prix – Monte Carlo

1st Alain Prost – McLaren-TAG
2nd Ayrton Senna – Toleman-Hart
3rd Stefan Bellof – Tyrell-Ford
In the pouring rain Senna drove brilliantly to finish 2nd. After qualifying 13th he had risen to 9th by the end of the Lap 1 and was 7th on Lap 7. He then began to pick off the leaders, and by Lap 30 was 2nd, challenging Prost until the race was stopped on Lap 32; he took his first fastest lap.

17 June – Canadian Grand Prix – Montreal

1st Nelson Piquet – Brabham-BMW
2nd Niki Lauda – McLaren-TAG
3rd Alain Prost – McLaren-TAG
Senna qualified 9th on the grid, his first time in the top ten; he finished 7th, two laps behind the leaders.

24 June – United States Grand Prix – Detroit

1st Nelson Piquet – Brabham-BMW
2nd Elio de Angelis – Lotus-Renault
3rd Teo Fabi – Brabham-BMW
Senna had to start the race in the spare car after a start line shunt. He had qualified 7th and was leading the pack of 'young lions', Brundle, Boutsen and Bellof, when a front wishbone broke on Lap 21 and he crashed spectacularly.

8 July – Dallas Grand Prix

1st Keke Rosberg – Williams-Honda
2nd Rene Arnoux – Ferrari
3rd Elio de Angelis – Lotus-Renault
Senna qualified in 6th on the grid, but had squeezed into 4th place by the end of Lap 1. Then he touched a wall and spun. Having changed tyres, he did the same thing again. On Lap 47 he retired with a broken driveshaft.

15 July – World Sportscar Endurance Championships – Nurburgring

Driving Porsche 956 with Henri Pescarolo and Stefan Johansson

1st Stefan Bellof/Derek Bell
      Porsche 956-83
2nd Thierry Boutsen/David Hobbs
      Porsche 956-83
3rd Sandro Nannini/Jan Lammers
      Porsche 956-83

It was Senna's first race in a closed racing car. Pescarolo, Johansson and Senna ran in the top ten until the clutch packed up and they lost eight laps; they eventually finished 7th.

22nd July – British Grand Prix – Brands Hatch

1st Niki Lauda – McLaren-TAG
2nd Derek Warwick – Renault
3rd Ayrton Senna – Toleman-Hart
Senna's second podium finish. After qualifying 7th he pursued Elio de Angelis with persistence for much of the race and with five laps to go, surged past him on the inside to take 3rd place, bringing the crowd to its feet.

5 August – German Grand Prix – Hockenheim

1st Alain Prost – McLaren-TAG
2nd Niki Lauda – McLaren-TAG
3rd Derek Warwick – Renault
Senna qualified 9th and quickly rose to 5th place on Lap 5 when excessive vibration from the Toleman broke the rear wing and it spun backwards into a barrier.

19 August – Austrian Grand Prix – Osterreichring

1st Niki Lauda – McLaren-TAG
2nd Nelson Piquet – Brabham-BMW
3rd Michele Alboreto – Ferrari
Senna qualified 10th, and by Lap 14 was challenging Derek Warwick for fifth place. When Warwick went in for tyres, Senna held 5th until his engine expired on Lap 35 with oil pressure problems.

Dutch – Grand Prix – Zandvoort

1st Alain Prost – McLaren-TAG
2nd Niki Lauda – McLaren-TAG
3rd Nigel Mansell – Lotus-Renault
Senna qualified 13th, but his engine failed on Lap 19.

Italian – Grand Prix – Monza

1st Niki Lauda – McLaren-TAG
2nd Michele Alboreto – Ferrari
3rd Riccardo Patrese – Alfa-Romeo
Following his controversial deal with Lotus, Toleman suspended Senna so he did not start the race. Stefan Johansson, driving in Senna's place, finished 4th.

7 October – European Grand Prix – Nurburgring

1st Alain Prost – McLaren-TAG
2nd Michele Alboreto – Ferrari
3rd Nelson Piquet – Brabham-BMW
Senna qualified 12th but went into the back of Rosberg on Lap 1 and retired. He claimed he had been squeezed out, but others suggested he had braked too late.

21 October – Portuguese Grand Prix – Estoril

1st Alain Prost – McLaren-TAG
2nd Niki Lauda – McLaren-TAG
3rd Ayrton Senna – Toleman-Hart
In the final race of the season Senna qualified 3rd on the grid, and after dropping back to 4th, overtook Rosberg on Lap 19 to regain 3rd place.

1985
Lotus 97T-Renault

7 April – Brazilian Grand Prix – Rio de Janeiro
1st Alain Prost – McLaren-TAG
2nd Michele Alboreto – Ferrari
3rd Elio de Angelis – Lotus-Renault
Senna qualified 4th and held 3rd place for much of the race. Recognizing that his conservative tyre choice and poor fuel consumption prevented him from winning, he drove a mature race, but was forced to retire on Lap 49 when the engine failed, much to the disappointment of the home crowd.

21 April – Portuguese Grand Prix – Estoril
1st Ayrton Senna – Toleman-Hart
2nd Michele Alboreto – Ferrari
3rd Patrick Tambay – Renault
Senna's first pole position, and his first Grand Prix victory. In torrential rain he led from the start, demonstrating a level of control that was to become his hallmark; he also took the fastest lap.

5 May – San Marino Grand Prix – Imola
1st Elio de Angelis – Lotus-Renault
2nd Thierry Boutsen – Arrows-BMW
3rd Patrick Tambay – Renault
Senna's second pole position; he dominated the race until, with four laps to go, he ran out of fuel. Prost won on the circuit, but was disqualified for being under the weight limit and Elio de Angelis, Senna's team mate, was declared the winner.

19 May – Monaco Grand Prix – Monte Carlo
1st Alain Prost – McLaren-TAG
2nd Michele Alboreto – Ferrari
3rd Elio de Angelis – Lotus-Renault
Senna's third pole position in a row, but during the race warm-up he inadvertently over-revved the engine after changing from fifth to second and although he led for the first thirteen laps the engine expired.

17 June – Canadian Grand Prix – Montreal
1st Michele Alboreto–- Ferrari
2nd Stefan Johansson – Ferrari
3rd Alain Prost – McLaren-TAG
Senna qualified 2nd, but on Lap 6 he came into the pits complaining of a lack of turbo boost pressure. It was a loose pipe, and while it was being fixed he lost five laps; back in the race, he broke the lap record, but could only finish 16th.

23 June – United States Grand Prix – Detroit
1st Keke Rosberg – Williams-Honda
2nd Stefan Johansson – Ferrari
3rd Michele Alboreto – Ferrari
Senna took pole position and jostled with Mansell for the lead before establishing himself in front. By Lap 7 his choice of tyres was proving troublesome, so he came in and returned in 14th place; he then set fastest lap, and by Lap 53 was challenging Johansson for second place when he hit a wall.

7 July – French Grand Prix – Paul Ricard
1st Nelson Piquet – Brabham-BMW
2nd Keke Rosberg – Williams-Honda
3rd Alain Prost – McLaren-TAG
Senna qualified in 2nd place but lost it to Piquet on Lap 4. Third gear on the Lotus then began to stick, sending Senna into the pits on Lap 9; he returned a lap behind the leaders. As he climbed through the midfield his engine blew up spectacularly on Lap 27 and he spun on his own oil, crashing into a barrier.

21 July – British Grand Prix – Silverstone

1st Alain Prost – McLaren-TAG
2nd Michele Alboreto – Ferrari
3rd Jacquest Laffite – Ligier-Renault
This race should have been Senna's. After qualifying 4th he made a brilliant start and stormed into the lead, fighting off a challenge from Keke Rosberg. By Lap 14 he had pulled out a lead of several seconds, then Prost challenged, putting enormous pressure on Senna to use boost, and fuel, to get on even terms; after twelve laps of duelling with Prost, his electronic fuel injection failed.

4 August – German Grand Prix – Nurbergring

1st Michele Alboreto – Ferrari
2nd Alain Prost – McLaren-TAG
3rd Jacques Laffite – Ligier-Renault
Once again the Lotus let him down; having qualified 5th he moved up to 2nd as Johansson made contact with Alboreto on the first lap. By Lap 10 Rosberg and Senna were pulling away from the field, and on Lap 15 Senna took the lead, then on Lap 27 a driveshaft constant velocity joint overheated and the engine failed, the fourth race in a row he had failed to finish.

European Grand Prix, 1985

18 August – Austrian Grand Prix – Osterreichring

1st Alain Prost – McLaren-TAG
2nd Ayrton Senna – Lotus-Renault
3rd Michele Alboreto – Ferrari
Despite qualifying 14th, Senna climbed to 7th by Lap 8. As the leading cars dropped out, he inherited 3rd place on Lap 27, but experienced severe vibrations which were so bad that he took one hand off the steering wheel whenever he could; when Lauda's engine expired on Lap 40 he inherited 2nd place, where he finished.

25 August – Dutch Grand Prix – Zandvoort

1st Niki Lauda – McLaren-TAG
2nd Alain Prost – McLaren-TAG
3rd Ayrton Senna – Lotus-Renault
Senna qualified 4th and quickly moved into 2nd behind Rosberg. Rosberg then retired, and Prost passed Senna into the lead. Senna dropped down to 3rd as Lauda and Prost fought it out and remained there despite a stiff challenge from Alboreto.

8 September – Italian Grand Prix – Monza

1st Alain Prost – McLaren-TAG
2nd Nelson Piquet – Brabham-BMW
3rd Ayrton Senna – Lotus-Renault

Senna took pole position, but during the race he slipped to 4th, hampered by fuel consumption and engine problems, and was unable to prevent Nelson Piquet's progress. When Rosberg retired with eight laps to go, Senna inherited 3rd and was back on the podium.

15 September – Belgian Grand Prix – Spa

1st Ayrton Senna – Lotus-Renault
2nd Nigel Mansell – Williams-Honda
3rd Alain Prost – McLaren-TAG
After qualifying 2nd, Senna took the lead and stayed there, excluding pit stops, for the whole race. Tricky conditions enabled him to give a dazzling display of car control and take his second victory of the season. The track went from wet to dry, with a shower in the middle.

6 October – European Grand Prix – Brands Hatch

1st Nigel Mansell – Williams-Honda
2nd Ayrton Senna – Lotus-Renault
3rd Keke Rosberg – Williams-Honda
Senna took pole position but was outpaced by Nigel Mansell, for whom this was his first Grand Prix victory. After jousting with Mansell in the opening lap, Senna was blocked by Mansell's team mate Rosberg in order to let Mansell

through. Senna settled for 2nd place before being overtaken by Marc Surer and Jacques Laffite who later dropped back; then Surer's engine blew up and Senna's 2nd place was assured.

19 October – South African Grand Prix – Kyalami

1st Nigel Mansell – Williams-Honda
2nd Keke Rosberg – Williams-Honda
3rd Alain Prost – McLaren-TAG
Senna qualified 4th and was holding it when his engine expired on Lap 9; the Williams-Hondas of Mansell and Rosberg were again dominant.

3 November – Australian Grand Prix – Adelaide

1st Keke Rosberg – Williams-Honda
2nd Jacques Laffite – Ligier-Renault
3rd Philippe Streiff – Ligier-Renault
In the first Australian Grand Prix Senna took pole position and fought a terrific battle with Rosberg at Victoria Park; it was one of his most erratic performances, involving several unruly incidents, the first of which, on the opening lap, involved his forcing Nigel Mansell on to the kerb, effectively finishing his race. Senna was leading on Lap 60 when his engine blew up and he trailed into the pits.

1986
Lotus 98T-Renault

23 March – Brazilian Grand Prix – Rio de Janeiro

1st Nelson Piquet – Williams-Honda
2nd Ayrton Senna – Lotus-Renault
3rd Jacques Laffite – Ligier-Renault
Senna took pole position but it was clear from the race warm-up that the Lotus 98T could not compete with the Williams-Honda on fuel consumption. On the first lap Senna had several close encounters with Mansell, as the Englishman tried to overtake and spun off.

13 April – Spanish Grand Prix – Jerez

1st Ayrton Senna – Lotus-Renault
2nd Nigel Mansell – Williams-Honda
3rd Alain Prost – McLaren-TAG
Senna took pole position and led until Mansell got the better of him; Mansell's tyres then started to wear, and when Senna went past, with just eight laps to go, Mansell went into the pits. He emerged 19.4 seconds behind Senna but somehow caught him and on the final straight he drew practically level as they crossed the finishing line. Senna had won a classic race by the narrowest of margins, 0.014 seconds.

27 April – San Marino Grand Prix – Imola

1st Alain Prost – McLaren-TAG
2nd Nelson Piquet – Williams-Honda
3rd Gerhard Berger – Benetton-BMW
Senna took pole position but Piquet overtook him on the first lap. A vibration from the rear of the car caused him to drop back to 4th, then on Lap 11 the right rear wheel-bearing broke and he retired.

11 May – Monaco Grand Prix – Monte Carlo

1st Alain Prost – McLaren-TAG
2nd Keke Rosberg – McLaren-TAG
3rd Ayrton Senna – Lotus-Renault
Senna started 3rd, behind Prost and Mansell, but passed Mansell on the first lap; he was unable to catch Prost though and was eventually caught by Rosberg on Lap 42 when he went in for tyres.

25 May – Belgian Grand Prix – Spa

1st Nigel Mansell – Williams-Honda
2nd Ayrton Senna – Lotus-Renault
3rd Stefan Johansson – Ferrari
From 4th place on the grid, Senna caused chaos when he tried to overtake Berger and Prost as they went round La Source corner. Cars sprayed left and right to avoid the airborne Prost, but when things

settled down, Senna was 2nd behind Piquet. Mansell passed him, then dropped back, and when Piquet retired on Lap 16, Senna briefly led. Mansell re-took him after a tyre stop.

15 June – Canadian Grand Prix – Montreal

1st Nigel Mansell – Williams-Honda
2nd Alain Prost – McLaren-TAG
3rd Nelson Piquet – Williams-Honda
Senna started 2nd on the grid, and remained there until he slid off while Prost was overtaking him on Lap 4. From 6th, he moved up one place at the expense of Rene Arnoux to finish 5th.

22 June – United States Grand Prix – Detroit

1st Ayrton Senna – Lotus-Renault
2nd Jacques Laffite – Ligier-Renault
3rd Alain Prost – McLaren-TAG
Senna took pole position, but on Lap 12 a puncture brought him in and he rejoined in 8th place. He regained the lead on Lap 36 with a brilliant drive. Then Prost had an intermittent cut-out, Piquet crashed, Arnoux ran into the wreckage and Mansell hobbled in fifth – he won, and suddenly he was leading the World Championship.

6 July – French Grand Prix – Paul Ricard

1st Nigel Mansell – Williams-Honda
2nd Alain Prost – McLaren-TAG
3rd Nelson Piquet – Williams-Honda
Senna took pole position but Mansell overtook him on the opening straight. On Lap 4 the Minardi of Andrea de Cesaris spewed oil all over the track on which Senna spun in on Lap 5, hit a barrier and smashed a front wheel. He went straight back to the pits and apologised to the Lotus mechanics.

13 July – British Grand Prix – Brands Hatch

1st Nigel Mansell – Williams-Honda
2nd Nelson Piquet – Williams-Honda
3rd Alain Prost – McLaren-TAG
Senna qualified 4th, and after a restart was down to 5th before rising to 3rd. But his Lotus was no match for the Williams-Hondas, and when fourth gear broke on Lap 27 he retired.

27 July – German Grand Prix – Hockenheim

1st Nelson Piquet – Williams-Honda
2nd Ayrton Senna – Lotus-Renault
3rd Nigel Mansell – Williams-Honda
Senna qualified 3rd on the grid, then led on the first lap; on the second lap Rosberg nipped past him, then Piquet, and by Lap 6 Prost had passed him too. Rosberg ran out of fuel as did Prost a few hundred yards before the finishing line, and though Prost tried to push his McLaren across the line, Senna sailed past to take 2nd.

10 August – Hungarian Grand Prix – Hungaroring

1st Nelson Piquet – Williams-Honda
2nd Ayrton Senna – Lotus-Renault
3rd Nigel Mansell – Williams-Honda
The first Hungarian Grand Prix saw Senna in pole position and leading until Piquet eased past him on Lap 12. Senna hung on, and regained the lead by a judicious tyre change on Lap 42, and a fantastic duel then ensued with Piquet and Senna racing wheel-to-wheel until Lap 57 when Piquet pulled away from Senna, shaking his fist as he went past. Senna's 2nd place put him second in the World Championship.

European Grand Prix, 1986

17 August – Austrian Grand Prix – Osterreichring
1st Alain Prost – McLaren-TAG
2nd Michele Alboreto – Ferrari
3rd Stefan Johansson – Ferrari
Senna could only manage 8th on the grid, and had to change a blistered tyre on Lap 8 and after mechanical problems he retired on Lap 13.

7 September – Italian Grand Prix – Monza
1st Nelson Piquet – Williams-Honda
2nd Nigel Mansell – Williams-Honda
3rd Stefan Johansson – Ferrari
Senna qualified 5th, but retired on the start line with failed transmission.

21 September – Portuguese Grand Prix – Estoril
1st Nigel Mansell – Williams-Honda
2nd Alain Prost – McLaren-TAG
3rd Nelson Piquet – Williams-Honda
Senna took pole position and was lying 2nd on the last lap when his Lotus ran out of fuel; he was classified 4th although he did not officially complete the distance.

26 October – Australian Grand Prix – Adelaide

1st Alain Prost – McLaren-TAG
2nd Nelson Piquet – Williams-Honda
3rd Stefan Johansson – Ferrari

Despite qualifying 3rd, Senna's Lotus was quickest in the morning warm-up, but after losing 3rd to Mansell on Lap 4, he experienced engine problems and Prost overtook him a few laps later. Senna's engine finally blew up on Lap 43.

1987
Lotus 99T-Honda

12 April – Brazilian Grand Prix – Rio de Janeiro

1st Alain Prost – McLaren-TAG
2nd Nelson Piquet – Williams-Honda
3rd Stefan Johansson – McLaren-TAG

Senna qualified 3rd and when Piquet went in on Lap 7 he briefly led the race for two laps. Handling problems then forced him into the pits, after which he stormed back to second place on Lap 39, but retired on Lap 50 with a broken separator in his oil tank.

12 October – Mexican Grand Prix – Mexico City

1st Gerhard Berger – Benetton-BMW
2nd Alain Prost – McLaren-TAG
3rd Ayrton Senna – Lotus-Renault

From pole position Senna was overtaken by Piquet on the first corner. He led briefly on Lap 30, when Piquet went in for new tyres, but he then did the same on Lap 36 and Berger went through to win the race. Senna made a second stop for tyres during which Prost passed him, but in trying to beat Prost, Senna wore his tyres down and finished with them badly blistered.

3 May – San Marino Grand Prix – Imola

1st Nigel Mansell – Williams-Honda
2nd Ayrton Senna – Lotus-Honda
3rd Michele Alboreto – Ferrari
Senna took pole position but was overtaken by Mansell. Senna eventually won the battle for second place after seeing off Patrese and Alboreto.

17 May – Belgian Grand Prix – Spa

1st Alain Prost – McLaren-TAG
2nd Stefan Johansson – McLaren-TAG
3rd Andrea de Cesaris –
    Brabham-BMW
Another pole position for Senna, but he touched wheels with Mansell when fighting for the lead and they both spun off. Mansell later grabbed him in the pits and had to be restrained by mechanics.

31 May – Monaco Grand Prix – Monte Carlo

1st Ayrton Senna – Lotus-Honda
2nd Nelson Piquet – Williams-Honda
3rd Michele Alboreto – Ferrari
Senna was handed victory when Mansell, who had led from the start, retired on Lap 30 with turbo boost failure. It was Senna's first victory in the Lotus 99T.

21 June – United States Grand Prix – Detroit

1st Ayrton Senna – Lotus-Honda
2nd Nelson Piquet – Williams-Honda
3rd Alain Prost – McLaren-TAG
Senna qualified 2nd and pursued Mansell for fifteen laps until he experienced braking problems. He then nursed the Lotus until Mansell experienced first a disastrous tyre stop and then cramps in the upper body and could only finish 5th. Senna won without changing tyres and took fastest lap.

5 July – French Grand Prix – Paul Ricard

1st Nigel Mansell – Williams-Honda
2nd Nelson Piquet – Williams-Honda
3rd Alain Prost – McLaren-TAG
Senna, leading the World Championship, was completely outpaced by the Williams-Hondas of Mansell and Nelson Piquet, despite sharing the same engine. His disappointing 4th merely emphasized the weakness of the Lotus.

12 July – British Grand Prix – Silverstone

1st Nigel Mansell – Williams-Honda
2nd Nelson Piquet – Williams-Honda
3rd Ayrton Senna – Lotus-Honda
Senna was again outpaced by the power of the Williams-Hondas and could only watch as they took another 1–2. He won his battle for third place with Prost when the Frenchman's clutch failed and he had to retire.

26 July – German Grand Prix – Hockenheim

1st Nelson Piquet – Williams-Honda
2nd Stefan Johansson – McLaren-TAG
3rd Ayrton Senna – Lotus-Honda
Senna was lucky to manage 3rd after a number of mechanical mishaps. His Lotus lost all the hydraulic fluid from its active suspension and sagged on to its secondary 'reserve' springs, but he limped round to come in 3rd.

9 August – Hungarian Grand Prix – Hungaroring

1st Nelson Piquet – Williams-Honda
2nd Ayrton Senna – Lotus-Honda
3rd Alain Prost – McLaren-TAG
Senna struggled against an occasionally jumping fourth gear to come 2nd after Mansell had led the race and retired.

16 August – Austrian Grand Prix – Osterreichring

1st Nigel Mansell – Williams-Honda
2nd Nelson Piquet – Williams-Honda
3rd Teo Fabi – Benetton-Ford

Senna qualified 7th and at one stage dropped down to 9th after a clash with his old rival Michele Alboreto forced him into the pits for a new nose section; he finished 5th, two laps behind Mansell.

6 September – Italian Grand Prix – Monza

1st Nelson Piquet – Williams-Honda
2nd Ayrton Senna – Lotus-Honda
3rd Nigel Mansell – Williams-Honda
Senna grabbed the lead on Lap 24 after qualifying 4th and held it until Lap 43 when he slid off at the Parabolica with worn tyres; he managed to restart and finish 2nd.

20 September – Portuguese Grand Prix – Estoril

1st Alain Prost – McLaren-TAG
2nd Gerhard Berger – Ferrari
3rd Nelson Piquet – Williams-Honda
Senna, having qualified 5th, found himself in last place at the end of Lap 14 when throttle problems forced him into the pits. From then on he drove like the wind and eventually finished 7th.

27 September – Spanish Grand Prix – Jerez

1st Nigel Mansell – Williams-Honda
2nd Alain Prost – McLaren-TAG
3rd Stefan Johansson – McLaren-TAG

An aggressive drive from Senna took him from 5th place on the grid to 2nd place on the circuit. Without changing tyres, he held it against a succession of drivers including Alboreto, Boutsen and Piquet, until Lap 63 when he finally had to give way; he finished 5th.

18 October – Mexican Grand Prix – Mexico City

1st Nigel Mansell – Williams-Honda
2nd Nelson Piquet – Williams-Honda
3rd Riccardo Patrese – Brabham-BMW
Senna qualified 7th and managed to work his way up to 2nd despite having no clutch for most of the race. He was then overtaken by Piquet, locked his brakes and spun off on Lap 54. After arguing with officials over a push, he vented his rage on one of them and was later fined $15,000 for striking an official.

1 November – Japanese Grand Prix – Suzuka

1st Gerhard Berger – Ferrari
2nd Ayrton Senna – Lotus-Honda
3rd Stefan Johansson – McLaren-TAG
With the uncompetitive Lotus, Senna could only qualify 7th but immediately sped into 4th place, ahead of Nelson Piquet. The two Brazilians then raced for 3rd place

until Piquet's engine blew up. Senna then overtook Johansson on the last lap, to take 2nd.

15 November – Australian Grand Prix – Adelaide

1st Gerhard Berger – Ferrari
2nd Michele Alboreto – Ferrari
3rd Thierry Boutsen –
    Benetton-Ford
Senna qualified 4th, then overtook Prost and Alboreto in a daring move for second place, then challenged Berger for the lead for the remainder of the race. However, after a protest from Benetton, scrutineers ruled the extra brake cooling ducts fitted to the Lotus illegal and Senna was disqualified, a sad end to his Lotus career.

1988
McLaren MP4/4 Honda

3 April – Brazilian Grand Prix – Rio de Janeiro

1st Alain Prost – McLaren-Honda
2nd Gerhard Berger – Ferrari
3rd Nelson Piquet – Lotus-Honda
The beginning of a dominant period for McLaren with the new Honda turbos, Senna took pole position in his first race for them, then he had gear-linkage derangement and had to switch cars. Starting from the pit

lane he raced through the field to 2nd place when his battery went flat. After restarting in 6th place, he was disqualified on Lap 31 for having changed cars illegally at the start of the race.

1 May – San Marino Grand Prix – Imola

1st Ayrton Senna – McLaren-Honda
2nd Alain Prost – McLaren-Honda
3rd Nelson Piquet – Lotus-Honda
Senna took pole position and led from the start as Prost became engulfed in the pack. By the time he had emerged into 2nd place, Senna was a long way ahead. The two lapped the rest of the field, but Senna finished comfortably ahead.

15 May – Monaco Grand Prix – Monte Carlo

1st Alain Prost – McLaren-Honda
2nd Gerhard Berger – Ferrari
3rd Michele Alboreto – Ferrari
Senna took pole position and fastest lap and led until Lap 67 when he inexplicably hit a barrier. His error was only a matter of inches but was enough to put him out of the race and cause him a huge amount of embarrassment. He explained later that his right front wheel had tapped the inside barrier and the impact had jolted the steering wheel from his hands.

Monaco Grand Prix, 1987

29 May – Mexican Grand Prix – Mexico City

1st Alain Prost McLaren-Honda
2nd Ayrton Senna – McLaren-Honda
3rd Gerhard Berger – Ferrari
Senna took pole position but was beaten to the corner by Prost. After being overtaken by Piquet, he regained 2nd place but by that time Prost was well ahead. Understeer caused tyre wear and he was also suffering from unexpectedly high fuel consumption and he finished 2nd.

12 June – Canadian Grand Prix – Montreal

1st Ayrton Senna – McLaren-Honda
2nd Alain Prost – McLaren-Honda
3rd Thierry Boutsen – Benetton-Ford
The longest race of the year. Senna and Prost quickly took total control, Senna took pole position and fastest lap, out-manoeuvring Prost. The only concern for McLaren was fuel consumption; and they instructed their drivers to reduce boost.

19 June – United States Grand Prix – Detroit

1st Ayrton Senna – McLaren-Honda
2nd Alain Prost – McLaren-Honda
3rd Theirry Boutsen – Benetton-Ford

After taking pole position, Senna led from start to finish on a circuit that Prost disliked. Once again they lapped the rest of the field of normally aspirated cars. Prost now had 45 points in the World Championship to Senna's 33.

3 July – French Grand Prix – Paul Ricard

1st Alain Prost – McLaren-Honda
2nd Ayrton Senna – McLaren-Honda
3rd Michele Alboreto – Ferrari
On Prost's home circuit there was not much to distinguish the two McLaren drivers. Senna was struggling with a gearbox problem and qualified 2nd; he then chased Prost for thirty-four laps and decided to change tyres first. When Prost changed tyres, Senna got in front, but finally, on Lap 61, Prost went past in a brilliant overtaking manoeuvre as Senna was boxed in behind Pierluigi Martini's Minardi.

10 July – British Grand Prix – Silverstone

1st Ayrton Senna – McLaren-Honda
2nd Nigel Mansell Williams–Judd
3rd Alessandro Nannini – Benetton-Ford
It was the first time this season that a McLaren-Honda had not led the first lap. Senna could only manage

3rd on the grid with Prost 4th. In the pouring rain Gerhard Berger led for fourteen laps in the fuel-guzzling Ferrari before Senna caught him. Prost, unhappy in the wet, gave up on Lap 24.

24 July – German Grand Prix – Hockenheim

1st Ayrton Senna – McLaren-Honda
2nd Alain Prost – McLaren-Honda
3rd Gerhard Berger – Ferrari
After taking pole position, Senna triumphed in atrocious weather. Prost had a poor start and he later spun; he managed to challenge Senna briefly for the lead before settling for second. Senna was 3 points behind him in the World Championship.

8 August – Hungarian Grand Prix – Hungaroring

1st Ayrton Senna – McLaren-Honda
2nd Alain Prost – McLaren-Honda
3rd Thierry Boutsen –
    Benetton-Ford
Senna took pole and led until Lap 49 when Prost smartly dodged inside him while they were lapping backmarkers Tarquini and Alliot. Prost held the lead for 30 yards before skidding and allowing Senna to slip back past him again to win, putting them level on points.

28 August – Belgian Grand Prix – Spa

1st Ayrton Senna – McLaren-Honda
2nd Alain Prost – McLaren-Honda
3rd Ivan Capelli – March-Judd
Senna took pole position but was delayed fractionally by wheel spin at the start. He then stormed past Prost mid-way through the first lap and from then on the race was his, his seventh Grand Prix win of the season.

11 September – Italian Grand Prix – Monza

1st Gerhard Berger – Ferrari
2nd Michele Alboreto – Ferrari
3rd Eddie Cheever – Arrows-Megatron
Senna took pole position, setting a new record of nine in one season, but was out of the race with two laps to go in a collision with Jean-Louis Schlesser, who was deputizing for Mansell in the Williams. The incident was controversial, many blaming Senna for trying to overtake Schlesser after coming under sustained pressure from the Ferraris of Berger and Alboreto.

25 September – Portuguese Grand Prix – Estoril

1st Alain Prost – McLaren-Honda
2nd Ivan Capelli – March-Judd
3rd Thierry Boutsen –
    Benetton-Ford
Portugal put a dent in Senna's Championship hopes. He lost pole position to Prost and struggled with fuel and oversteer problems. But worst of all was Prost's apparent rejuvenation. At the end of the first lap, after gaining the lead, a hint of desperation crept into Senna's driving as Prost tried to overtake him on the straight. Senna pushed him within a fraction of the pit wall. Prost was incensed by this act of what he saw as madness; Senna finished in 6th place.

2 October – Spanish Grand Prix – Jerez

1st Alain Prost – McLaren-Honda
2nd Nigel Mansell – Williams-Judd
3rd Alessandro Nannini –
    Benetton-Ford
Senna took pole position but had problems with his fuel gauge which read minus for much of the race. Prost drove a faultless race and Senna was 4th. Senna now trailed Prost by 5 points in the Championship but had more Grand Prix wins.

30 October – Japanese Grand Prix – Suzuka

1st *Ayrton Senna – McLaren-Honda*
2nd Alain Prost – McLaren–Honda
3rd Thierry Boutsen – Benetton-
    Ford

After taking pole position he stalled his engine and was 14th going into the first corner; at the end of the Lap 1 he was 8th, by Lap 16 he was 3rd and by Lap 27 he had overtaken Prost to gain the lead. From then on there was no challenge, Prost being slowed by gear problems. Senna clinched the World Championship, took fastest lap and broke the existing record of wins in one season with his eighth win of the year.

13 November – Australian Grand Prix – Adelaide

1st Alain Prost – McLaren-Honda
2nd Ayrton Senna – McLaren-Honda
3rd Nelson Piquet – Lotus-Honda

Senna took pole position, establishing a new record of thirteen in one season, but Prost got the jump on him on the sprint to the first chicane. Senna then suffered gearbox problems, and by Lap 65

Portuguese Grand Prix, 1988

he had lost second gear completely, crucial on the Adelaide circuit. McLaren's radio advice got him through and by increasing the fuel mixture he beat off the challenge of Piquet's Lotus to take 2nd.

1989
McLaren MP4/5 Honda

26 March – Brazilian Grand Prix – Rio de Janeiro
1st Nigel Mansell – Ferrari
2nd Alain Prost – McLaren-Honda
3rd Mauricio Gugelmin –
   March-Judd
In the first race of the season the new champion took pole position and was involved in a first-corner tangle with Berger's Ferrari. He then took four pit stops for tyres or body checks and finished 11th.

23 April – San Marino Grand Prix – Imola
1st Ayrton Senna – McLaren-Honda
2nd Alain Prost – McLaren-Honda
3rd Alessandro Nannini –
   Benetton-Ford
Pole position for Senna, but his relationship with Prost was damaged when Senna overtook him before the first corner. Prost said afterwards that an 'accord' had been broken and missed the post-race

press conference. Senna won, but from then on they did not speak except on team matters.

7 May – Monaco Grand Prix – Monte Carlo
1st Ayrton Senna – McLaren-Honda
2nd Alain Prost – McLaren-Honda
3rd Stefano Modena –
   Brabham-Judd
Senna took pole position and concealed the loss of first and second gears to outdrive Prost as the McLaren-Honda MP4/5s once again dominated. It was sweet revenge for Monaco the year before when he had lost to Prost after crashing into a barrier.

28 May – Mexican Grand Prix – Mexico City
1st Ayrton Senna – McLaren-Honda
2nd Riccardo Patrese –
   Williams-Renault
3rd Michele Alboreto – Tyrell-Ford
Senna's front of the grid at Mexico equalled Jim Clark's record of thirty-three pole positions. He won a tactical advantage by choosing harder 'B' compound tyres in the sweltering heat and when Prost tried to change to 'B's the McLaren team misunderstood and gave him one on the front left only; Prost finished 5th.

4 June – United States Grand Prix – Phoenix
1st Alain Prost – McLaren-Honda
2nd Riccardo Patrese –
   Williams-Renault
3rd Eddie Cheever – Arrows-Ford
Senna took pole position and fastest lap and led until he was forced to retire, misfiring, on Lap 34, giving Prost his first victory of the season.

18 June – Canadian Grand Prix – Montreal
1st Thierry Boutsen –
   Williams-Renault
2nd Riccardo Patrese –
   Williams-Renault
3rd Andrea de Cesaris –
   Dallara-Ford
The pouring rain produced another of Senna's great rain drives and an interesting race in which nineteen of the twenty-six starters did not finish. Senna, driving brilliantly, was leading with three laps to go when his engine failed.

9 July – French Grand Prix – Paul Ricard
1st Alain Prost – McLaren-Honda
2nd Nigel Mansell – Ferrari
3rd Riccardo Patrese –
   Williams-Renault
Senna started 2nd on the grid and after a restart his McLaren broke a

Mexican Grand Prix, 1989

spur gear and ground to a standstill before he reached the first corner. Prost coasted to victory.

16 July – British Grand Prix – Silverstone

1st Alain Prost – McLaren-Honda
2nd Nigel Mansell – Ferrari
3rd Alessandro Nannini –
      Benetton-Ford
Senna took pole position and was leading when he spun off on Lap 11 with a gearbox problem, his exit cheered by the British crowd. His fourth consecutive failure to finish left him 20 points behind Prost in the World Championship.

30 July – German Grand Prix – Hockenheim

1st Ayrton Senna – McLaren-Honda
2nd Alain Prost – McLaren-Honda
3rd Nigel Mansell – Ferrari
Senna took both pole position and fastest lap but lost the lead to Prost during tyre stops. He battled to catch Prost, but with three laps to go looked like finishing 2nd. Then Prost suddenly lost top gear and Senna stormed past to a much needed victory.

13 August – Hungarian Grand Prix – Hungaroring

1st Nigel Mansell – Ferrari
2nd Ayrton Senna – McLaren-Honda
3rd Thierry Boutsen –
      Williams-Renault
Senna chased Patrese for much of the race after the Italian had taken pole. When Patrese retired with a punctured radiator, Senna was in the lead, but not for long, as Mansell, who had driven from 12th on the grid to 2nd, outmanoeuvred him for a spectacular win.

27 August – Belgian Grand Prix – Spa

1st Ayrton Senna – McLaren-Honda
2nd Alain Prost – McLaren-Honda
3rd Nigel Mansell – Ferrari
On one of the most difficult circuits in the world, and in the pouring rain, Senna completed a masterful victory from pole position to chequered flag, putting him 11 points behind Prost in the World Championship.

10 September – Italian Grand Prix – Monza

1st Alain Prost – McLaren-Honda
2nd Gerhard Berger – Ferrari
3rd Thierry Boutsen –
      Williams-Renault

Senna led this race from the start having taken pole, a staggering 1.79 seconds ahead of his team mate Prost. But with nine laps to go his engine blew up, and Prost won.

24 September – Portuguese Grand Prix – Estoril

1st Gerhard Berger – Ferrari
2nd Alain Prost – McLaren-Honda
3rd Stefan Johansson – Onyx-Ford

Senna took pole position but was beaten on the first and subsequent laps by Berger. On Lap 48, Senna tried to overtake Mansell, who unbeknownst to him, was being black flagged for reversing in the pit lane; they collided, and Senna's race was over. Prost was 24 points ahead in the World Championship.

1 October – Spanish Grand Prix – Jerez

1st Ayrton Senna – McLaren-Honda
2nd Gerhard Berger – Ferrari
3rd Alain Prost - McLaren-Honda

Another pole position for Senna, who had been fined $20,000 for ignoring the black flag in qualifying.

He also took the fastest lap and won the race in imperious fashion.

22 October – Japanese Grand Prix – Suzuka

1st Alessandro Nannini – Benetton-Ford
2nd Riccardo Patrese – Williams-Renault
3rd Thierry Boutsen – Williams-Renault

Senna needed to win to keep his Championship hopes alive. He took pole position but was beaten at the start by Prost. On Lap 47, he tried to overtake and locked wheels with Prost as they approached the chicane. Prost got out, but Senna continued and crossed the line first, only to be disqualified because the marshals had pushed him; Prost had won the World Championship.

5 November – Australian Grand Prix – Adelaide

1st Thierry Boutsen – Williams-Renault
2nd Alessandro Nannini – Benetton-Ford
3rd Riccardo Patrese – Williams-Renault

Senna went to Adelaide protesting in vain against his disqualification at Suzuka. The race was a farcical end to the year: amidst torrential rain,

Senna took pole position but slammed into the back of Martin Brundle's Brabham on Lap 13 in a cloud of spume; Prost refused to drive.

1990
McLaren MP4/5B Honda

11 March – United States Grand Prix – Phoenix

1st Ayrton Senna – McLaren-Honda
2nd Jean Alesi – Tyrell-Ford
3rd Thierry Boutsen – Williams-Renault

Senna's victory at Phoenix was a mature, calculating one. Having been frustrated by mechanical problems during practice, and only qualifying 5th, he chased the young Frenchman Jean Alesi for much of the race and overtook him on Lap 33 only to be re-passed almost immediately. On the next lap he successfully got past Alesi again, where he stayed for the rest of the race.

25 March – Brazilian Grand Prix – Interlagos

1st Alain Prost – Ferrari
2nd Gerhard Berger – McLaren-Honda
3rd Ayrton Senna – McLaren-Honda

After taking pole position it looked like plain sailing for Senna at the revamped Interlagos circuit, but on Lap 44 a coming together with Saturo Nakajima damaged his nose cone; it was replaced, but with no chance of catching Prost, he had to be content with 3rd place.

13 May – San Marino Grand Prix – Imola

1st Riccardo Patrese – Williams-Renault

2nd Gerhard Berger – McLaren-Honda

3rd Alessandro Nannini – Benetton-Ford

Senna took pole position, but on Lap 4 a stone jammed in a brake caliper, split open a wheel rim and deflated a tyre, causing him to retire.

27 May – Monaco Grand Prix – Monte Carlo

1st Ayrton Senna – McLaren-Honda

2nd Jean Alesi – Tyrell-Ford

3rd Gerhard Berger – McLaren-Honda

Senna took pole position and led from the start. Alesi at one point looked like making a race of it, but was skewered by Berger, and when the race restarted was frustrated by Prost who then retired with mechanical trouble; Senna also took fastest lap.

10 June – Canadian Grand Prix – Montreal

1st Ayrton Senna – McLaren-Honda

2nd Nelson Piquet – Bentton-Ford

3rd Nigel Mansell – Ferrari

After taking pole, Senna never looked like being caught. A rain shower before the race helped but the rest of the field – Piquet, Mansell, Berger and Prost – were helpless as he dominated the race in familiar fashion.

24 June – Mexican Grand Prix – Mexico City

1st Alain Prost – Ferrari

2nd Nigel Mansell – Ferrari

3rd Gerhard Berger – McLaren-Honda

Senna had a 15-second lead when a slow puncture hit him on Lap 15. Instead of coming in for a tyre change he decided to chance it, and paid the price on Lap 63 when the tyre blew. Prost, having started 13th on the grid drove an exemplary race to come home ahead of Mansell.

8 July – French Grand Prix – Paul Ricard

1st Alain Prost – Ferrari

2nd Ivan Capelli – Leyton House-Judd

3rd Ayrton Senna – McLaren-Honda

The McLaren-Hondas were beginning to look tired. Although Senna and Berger initially led the race, after disastrous pit stops they never looked like challenging and the race was dominated by superb performances from Prost and Capelli. Senna now led Prost in the World Championship by 3 points.

15 July – British Grand Prix – Silverstone

1st Alain Prost – Ferrari

2nd Thierry Boutsen – Williams-Honda

3rd Ayrton Senna – McLaren-Honda

After an initial lead, Senna was overtaken by Mansell on Lap 13, spun on the next lap and found himself in 5th place. From then on he never looked like challenging the dominant Ferraris and was lucky to gain 3rd when Mansell retired. Prost now led the title race.

29 July – German Grand Prix – Hockenheim

1st Ayrton Senna – McLaren-Honda

2nd Alessandro Nannini – Benetton-Ford

3rd Gerhard Berger – McLaren-Ford

Power is the key at Hockenheim, and Senna was able to extract the maximum out of his McLaren MP4/5B after gaining pole position.

He was only challenged by Alessandro Nannini's Benetton-Ford, which he eventually overtook with nine laps to go. He was now joint-5th in the league table of all-time Grand Prix winners with his idol Juan-Manuel Fangio.

12 August – Hungarian Grand Prix – Hungaroring
1st Thierry Boutsen –
        Williams-Renault
2nd Ayrton Senna – McLaren-Honda
3rd Nelson Piquet – Benetton-Ford
Senna was involved in controversy as he unceremoniously bundled Alessandro Nannini off the circuit on Lap 64. Nannini might have won, but his retirement left the way for Boutsen to win a few feet ahead of Senna in a hard-fought race.

26 August – Belgian Grand Prix – Spa
1st Ayrton Senna – McLaren-Honda
2nd Alain Prost – Ferrari
3rd Gerhard Berger – McLaren-Honda
After haggling with McLaren over the renewal of his contract for 1991, Senna took pole position and confidently won with hardly a challenge. After a tyre change he managed to stay ahead of Nannini who was running non-stop, and he defeated Prost who now lagged

13 points behind in the World Championship.

9 September – Italian Grand Prix – Monza
1st Ayrton Senna – McLaren-Honda
2nd Alain Prost – Ferrari
3rd Gerhard Berger – McLaren-Honda
Senna's sixth win of the season followed pole position and fastest lap. Senna and Prost made a reconciliation of their long-running rivalry with a hand-shake.

23 September – Portuguese Grand Prix – Estoril
1st Nigel Mansell – Ferrari
2nd Ayrton Senna – McLaren-Honda
3rd Alain Prost – Ferrari
Senna was able to grab 2nd after a fracas between Prost and Mansell on the front row. His second World Championship now looked almost certain. Prost, who had been pushed back to 5th, never recovered in the race and was furious with Mansell.

30 September – Spanish Grand Prix – Jerez
1st Alain Prost – Ferrari
2nd Nigel Mansell – Ferrari
3rd Alessandro Nannini –
        Benetton-Ford

The weekend was overshadowed by the horrifying accident of Martin Donnelly who hit a barrier in practice at 147 mph. Senna visited the spot and later visited Donnelly in hospital. He responded by going out and taking his fiftieth pole position. In the race, however, he retired with a punctured radiator and engine problems on Lap 54.

21 October – Japanese Grand Prix – Suzuka
1st Nelson Piquet – Benetton-Ford
2nd Roberto Moreno –
        Benetton-Ford
3rd Aguri Suzuki – Lola-Lamborghini
The World Championship was decided on the first lap of Suzuka. Senna took pole position but went into the first corner determined to block Prost; they collided, ending the race for both of them.

4 November – Australian Grand Prix – Adelaide
1st Nelson Piquet – Benetton-Ford
2nd Nigel Mansell – Ferrari
3rd Alain Prost – Ferrari
Having again taken pole, Senna fought a wonderful battle with Mansell before missing second gear and crashing with twenty laps to go.

United States Grand Prix, 1990

1991
McLaren MP4/6 Honda

10 March – United States Grand Prix – Phoenix
1st *Ayrton Senna – McLaren-Honda*
2nd Alain Prost – Ferrari
3rd Nelson Piquet – Benetton-Ford
In the new V12 Honda-engined McLaren MP4/6, Senna simply outpaced Prost in the V12 Ferrari. Having taken pole position, Senna led from the start, though Prost still managed to come 2nd.

24 March – Brazilian Grand Prix – Interlagos
1st *Ayrton Senna – McLaren-Honda*
2nd Riccardo Patrese – Williams-Renault
3rd Gerhard Berger – McLaren-Honda
Senna, having taken pole, won the Brazilian Grand Prix at his eighth attempt, in a spectacular race that delighted his home crowd. Nigel Mansell pushed him hard from the start but eventually retired with gearbox trouble. Senna's car developed gearbox problems, losing third, then fifth and sixth, and at one point he had only neutral. Eventually he found sixth and stayed there to win, despite a rain shower

and the Williams of Patrese breathing down his neck. It was a brilliant victory of which he said: 'God gave me this race.'

28 April – San Marino Grand Prix – Imola
1st *Ayrton Senna – McLaren-Honda*
2nd Gerhard Berger – McLaren-Honda
3rd JJ Lehto – Dallara-Judd
The McLarens of Senna and Berger dominated the race, lapping all eight finishers. Senna took pole position and although Patrese led for the first ten laps, Senna got past him. All his major opponents – Patrese, Mansell, Alesi, Prost – retired.

12 May – Monaco Grand Prix – Monte Carlo
1st *Ayrton Senna – McLaren-Honda*
2nd Nigel Mansell – Williams-Renault
3rd Jean Alesi – Ferrari
Another pole position and Senna's fourth consecutive victory, again in dominant fashion; he led from start to finish, initially pursued by Tyrell's Stefano Modena, until he retired with a blown engine. Patrese also chased for a while before spinning on oil.

2 June – Canadian Grand Prix – Montreal
1st Nelson Piquet – Benetton-Ford
2nd Stefano Modena – Tyrell-Ford
3rd Riccardo Patrese – Williams-Renault
For the first time in the season, Senna and McLaren did not dominate. Senna qualified 3rd and retired on Lap 25 with alternator trouble.

16 June – Mexican Grand Prix – Mexico City
1st Riccardo Patrese – Williams-Renault
2nd Nigel Mansell – Williams-Renault
3rd *Ayrton Senna – McLaren-Honda*
Senna, outpaced by the Williams-Renaults of Mansell and Patrese, had to take a back seat as they battled for the lead. Driving a tactical race and showing a new maturity, he came 3rd, and began to express grave doubts about the competitiveness of the Honda RA 121E V12, 'Unless we change our own equipment pretty fast, we're going to have trouble later in the season.'

7 July – French Grand Prix – Magny Cours

1st Nigel Mansell –
       Williams-Renault
2nd Alain Prost – Ferrari
3rd Ayrton Senna – McLaren-Honda
Senna again trailed the Williams-Renault team, his problems were compounded by a faulty fuel computer, his 3rd place seem like a triumph.

14 July – British Grand Prix – Silverstone

1st Nigel Mansell –
       Williams-Renault
2nd Gerhard Berger – McLaren-Honda
3rd Alain Prost – Ferrari
After taking pole, but losing the lead to Mansell, Senna was briefly allowed to retake it before Mansell breezed past him on the Hangar straight. A dejected Senna was running 2nd when he ran out of fuel on the last lap, thanks to his persistently faulty fuel computer; he was 4th, but still had 51 points in the title race to Mansell's 33.

28 July – German Grand Prix – Hockenheim

1st Nigel Mansell –
       Williams-Renault
2nd Riccardo Patrese –
       Williams-Renault
3rd Jean Alesi – Ferrari

With Mansell again dominating, Senna's Championship lead was looking distinctly vulnerable. He was only 4th behind Patrese and Alesi when his Honda again ran out of fuel, leaving him 7th.

11 August – Hungarian Grand Prix – Hungaroring

1st Ayrton Senna – McLaren-Honda
2nd Nigel Mansell –
       Williams-Renault
3rd Riccardo Patrese –
       Williams-Renault
The Hungaroring saw a welcome return to the podium for Senna, his first victory in three months. With its unimaginative chicanes, overtaking was always difficult and once he had gained pole position he led from the start, fighting off challenges from Mansell and Patrese.

25 August – Belgian Grand Prix – Spa

1st Ayrton Senna – McLaren-Honda
2nd Gerhard Berger – McLaren-Honda
3rd Nelson Piquet – Benetton-Ford
Another superb victory for Senna against mechanical difficulties. Having taken pole, he was overtaken by Mansell who then retired with electrical failure. Similar failures for Alesi, de Cesaris and Patrese left Senna out in front

but struggling with gearchange problems similar to those in Brazil. With 71 points he was now 22 points ahead of Mansell.

8 September – Italian Grand Prix – Monza

1st Nigel Mansell –
       Williams-Renault
2nd Ayrton Senna – McLaren-Honda
3rd Alain Prost – Ferrari
Mansell had to win at Monza and he did. Having taken pole, Senna led for thirty-four laps but was eventually caught by Mansell who together with team mate Patrese, brilliantly piled the pressure on until Senna succumbed. Senna still managed fastest lap and his second place still gave him an 18-point lead in the Championship.

22 September – Portuguese Grand Prix – Estoril

1st Riccardo Patrese –
       Williams-Renault
2nd Ayrton Senna – McLaren-Honda
3rd Jean Alesi – Ferrari
Mansell's repeated ill luck lost him the Championship to Senna. Having been black flagged at Estoril in 1989, with twenty laps to go, the Williams pit crew made a mistake with his tyre change and a wheel came off. Patrese won, but 2nd

virtually sowed up the 1991 Championship for Senna.

29 September – Spanish Grand Prix – Barcelona

1st Nigel Mansell –
        Williams-Renault
2nd Alain Prost – Ferrari
3rd Riccardo Patrese –
        Williams-Renault

Senna made a critical error over choice of tyres before the race, and after a shower of rain shortly before the start, he spun on Lap 13; he finished 5th.

20 October – Japanese Grand Prix – Suzuka

Australian Grand Prix, 1991

1st Gerhard Berger – McLaren-Honda
2nd Ayrton Senna – McLaren-Honda

3rd Riccardo Patrese –
        Williams-Renault

Japan was once again the setting for the denouement of the World Championship. Mansell, who needed to win, spun off on Lap 9, leaving Senna and Berger to fight for it. With Mansell out, Senna allowed Berger to win; Senna had fastest lap.

3 November – Australian Grand Prix – Adelaide

1st Ayrton Senna – McLaren-Honda
2nd Nigel Mansell –
        Williams-Renault
3rd Gerhard Berger – McLaren-Honda

Another superlative performance from Senna. He took pole position and led until rain stopped the race on Lap 14.

1992
McLaren MP4/6B Honda

1 March – South African Grand Prix – Kyalami

1st Nigel Mansell –
        Williams-Renault
2nd Riccardo Patrese –
        Williams-Renault
3rd Ayrton Senna – McLaren-Honda

Senna could only watch at the new Kyalami circuit, the first South African Grand Prix for seven years, as Nigel Mansell sped off into the distance. The new Williams-Renault FW14B put the McLaren MP4/6B in the shade.

22 March – Mexican Grand Prix – Mexico City

1st Nigel Mansell –
        Williams-Renault
2nd Riccardo Patrese –
        Williams-Renault
3rd Michael Schumacher –
        Benetton-Ford

For the first time this season McLaren failed to get a driver on the first two rows of the grid and the McLaren MP4/6B looked well past its sell-by date in its last race. Senna still managed to hang on to third place until transmission failure stopped him on Lap 11.

McLaren MP4/7A Honda

5 April – Brazilian Grand Prix – Interlagos

1st Nigel Mansell –
    Williams-Renault

2nd Riccardo Patrese –
    Williams-Renault

3rd Michael Schumacher –
    Benetton-Ford

Things looked up for Senna in the new McLaren MP4/7A-Honda; he qualified 3rd on the grid, but during the race he was plagued by an intermittent engine cut-out and retired on Lap 17. It was the third Mansell-Patrese 1–2 in a row.

3 May – Spanish Grand Prix – Barcelona

1st Nigel Mansell –
    Williams-Renault

2nd Michael Schumacher –
    Benetton-Ford

3rd Jean Alesi – Ferrari

Another disappointment for Senna. His overenthusiasm got the better of him and he spun twice in his attempts to get past Michael Schumacher. Senna pressed Schumacher for 2nd place despite a lack of power from the McLaren, but he hit a wall with three laps to go.

17 May – San Marino Grand Prix – Imola

1st Nigel Mansell –
    Williams-Renault

2nd Riccardo Patrese –
    Williams-Renault

3rd Ayrton Senna – McLaren-Honda

Senna's hopes of retaining the Championship dwindled as Mansell recorded a record fifth straight victory. Senna struggled to finish 3rd, driving his below-par McLaren-Honda flat out, and he suffered from severe upper body cramps.

31 May – Monaco Grand Prix – Monte Carlo

1st Ayrton Senna – McLaren-Honda

2nd Nigel Mansell –
    Williams-Renault

3rd Riccardo Patrese –
    Williams-Renault

One of Senna's most exciting races. Mansell, starting from pole, led until, with seven laps to go, he had a slow puncture and came into the pits. Senna inherited the lead, and though frantically pursued by Mansell, who caught up with just three laps to go, Senna held on to the lead in the Monte Carlo streets to win by 0.215 seconds.

Monaco Grand Prix, 1992

167

14 June – Canadian Grand Prix – Montreal

1st Gerhard Berger – McLaren-Honda
2nd Michael Schumacher – Benetton-Ford
3rd Jean Alesi – Ferrari

Senna was handed the chance of a second victory on Lap 14 by one of Mansell's impulsive overtaking manoeuvres. The Englishman endeavoured to get past the Brazilian, who had qualified in pole position, and ploughed into a sand trap. But Senna was in turn frustrated on Lap 37 with an electrical failure, leaving his team mate Berger to take victory.

5 July – French Grand Prix – Magny Cours

1st Nigel Mansell – Williams-Renault
2nd Riccardo Patrese – Williams-Renault
3rd Martin Brundle – Benetton-Ford

Senna made a poor start, was overtaken by Berger and then got into a tangle with Schumacher on Lap 1, which put him out of the race with a stalled engine.

12 July – British Grand Prix – Silverstone

1st Nigel Mansell – Williams-Renault
2nd Riccardo Patrese – Williams-Renault
3rd Martin Brundle – Benetton-Ford

The old Formula Three rivalry with Martin Brundle flared up again as he and Senna battled for 3rd place for much of this race. Senna finally got past Brundle on Lap 52, only to succumb to transmission problems on the same lap.

26 July – German Grand Prix – Hockenheim

1st Nigel Mansell – Williams-Renault
2nd *Ayrton Senna – McLaren-Honda*
3rd Michael Schumacher – Benetton-Ford

The German Grand Prix saw great battles between Senna and Mansell and Senna and Patrese. When Mansell went in early for tyres Senna found himself in second place behind Patrese. Mansell came back and after several laps of dog-fighting was waved through by Senna who acknowledged the superior power of the Williams. He then found himself being pursued by Patrese who had also changed tyres. This time he did not give in, and Patrese

in his efforts to get past, spun off on the last lap.

16 August – Hungarian Grand Prix – Hungaroring

1st Ayrton Senna – McLaren-Honda
2nd Nigel Mansell – Williams-Renault
3rd Gerhard Berger – McLaren-Honda

Senna announced before the race that he had offered his services to Frank Williams for nothing for 1993. He was also banned from driving in England for a month, by Staines magistrates after being caught driving at 121 mph on the M25.

30 August – Belgian Grand Prix – Spa

1st Michael Schumacher – Benetton-Ford
2nd Nigel Mansell – Williams-Renault
3rd Riccardo Patrese – Williams-Renault

Senna, who qualified 2nd on the grid, battled to hang on to the lead on slicks as the rain came down, but was forced to change tyres on Lap 14, rejoining in 14th place; he finished 5th. Michael Schumacher scored his first Grand Prix victory.

13 September – Italian Grand Prix – Monza

1st Ayrton Senna – McLaren-Honda
2nd Martin Brundle – Benetton-Ford
3rd Michael Schumacher – Benetton-Ford

Ayrton Senna's third Grand Prix victory of the season was overshadowed by the decisions of Nigel Mansell and Honda to leave Formula One. Both Williams cars were uncharacteristically struck by failure of their hydraulic pump drivebelts, leaving Senna who qualified 2nd, to hold his old sparring partner Martin Brundle in 2nd place.

27 September – Portuguese Grand Prix – Estoril

1st Nigel Mansell – Williams-Renault
2nd Gerhard Berger – McLaren-Honda
3rd Ayrton Senna – McLaren-Honda

Senna, having made four pit stops, snatched 3rd place from Martin Brundle behind team mate Gerhard Berger. It was Nigel Mansell's ninth victory of the season, beating Senna's eight wins in 1988.

25 October – Japanese Grand Prix – Suzuka

1st Riccardo Patrese – Williams-Renault
2nd Gerhard Berger – McLaren-Honda
3rd Martin Brundle – Benetton-Ford

Senna retired on Lap 3 when his valvetrain system warning light came on. The race was dominated by Williams-Honda, and Mansell, having given the race to Patrese, had an engine failure.

8 November – Australian Grand Prix – Adelaide

1st Gerhard Berger – McLaren-Honda
2nd Michael Schumacher – Benetton-Ford
3rd Martin Brundle – Benetton-Ford

The most memorable part of this race was the duel between Mansell and Senna as both drivers vied for the lead at the beginning. Senna, attempting to get past Mansell on Lap 18, careered into the back of him, removing both from the race. Mansell, in his last Formula One race, bitterly criticized Senna, complaining of the failure of the stewards and Williams to take action.

1993
McLaren MP4/8 Ford

14 March – South African Grand Prix – Kyalami

1st Alain Prost – Williams-Renault
2nd Ayrton Senna – McLaren-Ford
3rd Mark Blundell – Ligier-Renault

A great wheel-to-wheel dog-fight between Senna and Prost. After qualifying 2nd on the grid, Senna outsprinted Prost to the first corner and Prost settled in 3rd behind Schumacher. On Lap 13 Prost overtook first Schumacher, then Senna and dominated the race as Senna experienced handling problems.

28 March – Brazilian Grand Prix – Interlagos

1st Ayrton Senna – McLaren-Ford
2nd Damon Hill – Williams-Renault
3rd Michael Schumacher – Benetton-Ford

A brilliant tactical victory for Senna. Prost and Hill in the Williams were steadily pulling away from him until a third of the way through the race, rain appeared. Prost delayed a tyre stop too long and aquaplaned into Emerson Fittipaldi. Hill led for a couple of laps then Senna, handling the wet weather on slicks, passed him to win.

*Brazlian Grand
Prix, 1993*

**9 May – Spanish Grand Prix –
Barcelona**

1st Alain Prost – Williams-Renault
2nd Ayrton Senna – McLaren-Ford
3rd Michael Schumacher –
        Benetton-Ford
Senna's 2nd place was a performance
of maturity in a race that was
unremarkable; Prost led from the
start pursued only by Hill whose
engine eventually failed.

**23 May – Monaco Grand Prix –
Monte Carlo**

1st Ayrton Senna – McLaren-Ford
2nd Damon Hill – Williams-Renault
3rd Jean Alesi – Ferrari
Senna's record-breaking sixth win
at Monaco was fortuitous. Having
crashed heavily in Thursday's
practice and driving with a bruised
wrist, he qualified 3rd but did not
look like defeating either Prost or
Schumacher. Prost was penalized
with a stop-go penalty for jumping
the start and he stalled twice in the
pit lane. Schumacher then
experienced hydraulic failure, and
with half the race over Senna found
himself in the lead.

**11 April – European Grand
Prix – Donington Park**

1st Ayrton Senna – McLaren-Ford
2nd Damon Hill – Williams-Renault
3rd Alain Prost – Williams-Renault
One of Senna's greatest drives in
the wet. After qualifying 4th,
Senna charged from 5th to 1st in the
opening lap and remained ahead for
the rest of the race, lapping all but
Hill, and changing tyres no fewer
than four times; he also took
fastest lap.

**25 April – San Marino Grand
Prix – Imola**

1st Alain Prost – Williams-Renault
2nd Michael Schumacher –
        Benetton-Ford
3rd Martin Brundle –
        Ligier-Renault
Prost, having gained pole position,
was initially overtaken by Hill and
Senna, but quickly regained the lead
on Lap 12 and remained there for
the rest of the race; Senna retired
with hydraulic failure on Lap 42.

13 June – Canadian Grand Prix – Montreal

1st Alain Prost – Williams-Renault
2nd Michael Schumacher –
    Benetton-Ford
3rd Damon Hill – Williams-Renault
Senna managed to hold on to 2nd
place until with seven laps to go he
retired with an alternator failure.
The race was again dominated by
Williams with Prost.

4 July – French Grand Prix – Magny Cours

1st Alain Prost – Williams-Renault
2nd Damon Hill – Williams-Renault
3rd Michael Schumacher –
    Benetton-Ford
Senna, in the inferior McLaren,
could only manage 4th while Alain
Prost gained his sixth French Grand
Prix win and the first Williams 1–2
of the season.

11 July – British Grand Prix – Silverstone

1st Alain Prost – Williams-Renault
2nd Michael Schumacher –
    Benetton-Ford
3rd Riccardo Patrese –
    Benetton-Ford
Senna retired in 5th place after
running out of fuel with one lap to
go. Alain Prost took his fiftieth
Grand Prix victory.

25 July – German Grand Prix – Hockenheim

1st Alain Prost – Williams-Renault
2nd Michael Schumacher –
    Benetton-Ford
3rd Mark Blundell – Ligier-Renault
Senna made a rare mistake on the
first lap, spinning in a tussle with
Prost; battling with a handling
problem Senna finished a
respectable 4th. Prost benefited
from Hill's misfortune when his
tyre deflated with two laps to go.

15 August – Hungarian Grand Prix – Hungaroring

1st Damon Hill – Williams-Renault
2nd Riccardo Patrese –
    Benetton-Ford
3rd Gerhard Berger – Ferrari
Senna, who had run 2nd to Hill,
retired early with throttle problems.
Hill won his first Grand Prix having
led from the start.

29 August – Belgian Grand Prix – Spa

1st Damon Hill – Williams-Renault
2nd Michael Schumacher –
    Benetton-Ford
3rd Alain Prost – Williams-Renault
Senna, after initially holding 3rd
place, came 4th. 'I enjoyed the first
few laps but after that I just couldn't
keep up,' he said.

12 September – Italian Grand Prix – Monza

1st Damon Hill – Williams-Renault
2nd Jean Alesi – Ferrari
3rd Michael Andretti –
    McLaren-Ford
Senna was boxed in 8th place at the
start, and in his anxiety to get past
Brundle's faster Ligier, ran
into the back of him on Lap 9.
Prost, aiming for his fourth
World Championship victory, was
frustrated when his engine blew up
with five laps to go.

26 September – Portuguese Grand Prix – Estoril

1st Michael Schumacher –
    Benetton-Ford
2nd Alain Prost – Williams-Renault
3rd Damon Hill – Williams-Renault
Senna's engine failed on Lap 19,
continuing his frustration with the
McLaren's lack of competitiveness.
For once the Williams team was
outraced by Schumacher and
Benetton, but Prost still clinched his
fourth World Championship.

24 October – Japanese Grand Prix – Suzuka

1st Ayrton Senna – McLaren-Ford
2nd Alain Prost – Williams-Renault
3rd Mika Hakkinen – McLaren-Ford
Senna's brilliant victory was his

fortieth Grand Prix win and McLaren's 103rd, equalling Ferrari's record. A mid-race shower set him up for victory after qualifying 2nd behind Prost. Victory was marred by a punch-up with Formula One debutant Eddie Irvine whom he accused of lack of respect.

7 November – Australian Grand Prix – Adelaide

1st Ayrton Senna – McLaren-Ford
2nd Alain Prost – Williams-Renault
3rd Damon Hill – Williams-Renault
Senna's last Grand Prix victory, his forty-first, and his last race with McLaren, giving them a record 104 wins. Starting on pole position he dominated the race, coming 2nd in the World Championship in an uncompetitive car.

1994
Williams FW16-Renault

27 March – Brazilian Grand Prix – Interlagos

1st Michael Schumacher – Benetton-Ford
2nd Damon Hill – Williams-Renault
3rd Jean Alesi – Ferrari
Senna took pole position and built up a lead of 4.5 seconds over 2nd placed Alesi. Schumacher got past Alesi, and by Lap 7 was 2.5 seconds behind Senna. On Lap 21 when Senna went in for tyres, Schumacher got past. Senna spun off on Lap 55, still trying to catch him.

17 April – Pacific Grand Prix – Aida, Japan

1st Michael Schumacher – Benetton-Ford
2nd Gerhard Berger – Ferrari
3rd Rubens Barrichello – Jordan-Hart
Senna took pole position but had too much wheel-spin at the start, allowing Schumacher past. Mika Hakkinen, clipped his rear and he spun; Nicola Larini crashed into Senna putting them both out of the race.

1 May – San Marino Grand Prix – Imola

1st Michael Schumacher – Benetton-Ford
2nd Nicola Larini – Ferrari
3rd Mika Hakkinen – McLaren-Peugeot
Senna took pole position for the sixty-fifth time in his career. A serious accident at the start brought out the safety car and when it went in on Lap 5 Senna was leading from Michael Schumacher. On Lap 7, his car left the track at Tamburello corner and hit the wall; he died in hospital later that day.

San Marino Grand Prix, 1994

ACKNOWLEDGEMENTS

JACKET
Front: ALL SPORT
Back left: EMPICS/HULTON
Back right top: COLOURSPORT
Back right bottom: COLOURSPORT

ALL SPORT/VANDYSTADT
14–15, 35, 36, 37, 63, 67, 70, 77, 79, 82–83, 98–99, 104–105,
106–107, 111, 112–113, 114–115, 117, 118–119, 128–129, 130,
142–143, 157, 159, 166, 167, 170, 172–173

AUTOSPORT
52, 61, 68–69, 72

COLOURSPORT/SIPA SPORT
30, 33, 34, 84–85, 86, 87, 89, 94, 102, 108, 109, 154, 162–163

EMPICS/HULTON DEUTSCH COLLECTION
9, 10–11, 13 (Reuter), 122, 124, 132–133

BEHRAM KAPADIA
74–75, 80, 90, 139, 146–147, 150–151

MERCEDES BENZ PRESS OFFICE
65, 126, 127

REX FEATURES/SIPA SPORT
26–27, 29

SUTTON PHOTOGRAPHIC
39, 41, 42–43, 44–45, 46–47, 49, 51, 53, 54, 56–57, 58, 59, 60

SYGMA
18, 20–21, 22, 24, 101

QUADRANT
125